The
British Railcar
AEC to HST

R. M. Tufnell

David & Charles
Newton Abbot   London   North Pomfret (Vt)

British Library Cataloguing in Publication Data

Tufnell, R. M.
  The British railcar.
  1. Railway motor-cars – Great Britain
  – History
  I. Title
  625.2   TF494

ISBN 0–7153–8529–1

Photoset in Plantin by
Northern Phototypesetting Co, Bolton
and printed in Great Britain
by Biddles Ltd, Guildford
for David & Charles (Publishers) Limited
Brunel House Newton Abbot Devon

Published in the United States of America
by David & Charles Inc.
North Pomfret Vermont 05053 USA

Contents

GWR railcar No 22, preserved in pre-second world war
livery with GWR 'shirt button' logo. (*R. H. G. Simpson*)

Introduction

What is a railcar? It could be defined as any powered rail vehicle that is not hauled by a separate locomotive. The term goes back much further than that of a motor car and was in use while people were making-up their minds whether to call that contraption a nonequine, an automobile or an autocar.

Originally all the rail applications were single-unit vehicles, but as soon as enough power was available trailers were added. Then railcars were coupled together, so that the DMU (diesel multiple-unit) came into being. Long before that there had been the EMU (electric multiple-unit) and to round off the system of nomenclature there is the DEMU (diesel-electric-multiple-unit) but that is only a variation of a DMU by reason of its transmission between the diesel power plant and the wheels.

Until 1968 the conventional train was one in which a steam locomotive hauled a number of individual coaches, which might have been one on a lightly used branch, or any number up to 15 (rarely more) on long distance express services. Obviously the locomotive had to be sufficiently powerful to haul the intended loads at sufficient speed to maintain time. Equally the number of coaches ought to have been adequate to carry the number of passengers presenting themselves. But some days were better than others; perhaps eight coaches would be enough on a particular service on one day but on others it might need twelve. Possibly a train would run over a long length of main line with a maximum load until portions were detached at junctions for branch destinations so that the express locomotive ran the final part of the journey with a featherweight load. With steam locomotives and, indeed, with an independent diesel or electric locomotive, the power is not sufficiently flexible to be related to a varying train formation. There are low power locomotives which would not have sufficient power to work heavy trains at high speed, and there are high power locomotives with far more installed power than needed to work a light train.

The railcar train is much more flexible. True the early steam and internal combustion railcars were limited in power output so that originally they could not haul additional vehicles at peak times. But as soon as multiple control was developed so that the diesel engines of several railcars coupled together could be controlled by one man in the leading cab, then the multiple-unit became a much more flexible train than its steam counterpart, since if several multiple-unit sets are coupled together each brings its own power plant and the power available is proportional to the weight of the train. This principle had been employed in electric trains from the early years of this century but was not seen until the late 1930s in internal combustion trains in Britain, largely because it was not until the early 1930s that the petrol or diesel train became a practical proposition. While there had been experiments in internal combustion traction from the end of the last century the main problem lay in the lack of a transmission suitable for rail traction use. Unlike a steam locomotive in which the pistons can apply full power from rest, the petrol or diesel engine does not have the torque to start under load and needs to be running at speed before it can move a load. A mechanical clutch and gearbox was adequate for cars, buses, and lorries but the early designs would not withstand heavy rail use. Electric transmissions in which the engine drove a generator powering electric motors were also tried but not with reliable success in heavy applications until the 1930s. Similarly with hydraulic transmission.

As will be seen in the following pages it was the Great Western Railway which brought the railcar into fleet service and developed it into multiple-unit form with twin railcar sets. Much of the work in these railcars formed the basis for the development of the British Railways multiple-unit programme of the 1950s with the Southern throwing in much of its electric traction experience to aid the development of diesel-electric trains. In 1960 came the first long distance express diesel trains, the diesel Blue Pullmans, luxury railcar trains indeed, but not originally equipped to multiple with each other; that came later. Today many services of non-electrified lines are worked with the fastest railcar of them all in BR regular service, the 125mph Inter-City 125 High Speed Trains. At the moment the Inter-City 125s are not equipped for multiple working since they operate on frequent headway services with fixed formations. There would be no technical reasons why they should not be so fitted but a pair forming 18 or 20 coach trains would fit into a few stations and are not required operationally. Thus the railcar train has come full circle from cheap substitute for steam to the principle non-electrified express type. This book looks at these railcar trains – that is the self-contained self-propelled train – and the variety of all those that came between.

Six-car dmu formation composed of two three-car Class
123 units on a Paddington–Oxford semi-fast working near
Pangbourne. (*British Rail*)

1 The early railcars

Steam Railcars

The railcar started in the steam age, and the earliest recorded model consisted of a 4-wheeled vehicle designed by James Samuel and built in 1847 by W. Bridges Adams at Fairfield Works, Bow, in East London. It was only 12ft 6in long and though officially called *Express* it was dubbed *Lilliputian*; it ran first from Shoreditch to Cambridge on the Eastern Counties Committee's line and eventually achieved over 5,500 miles in six months in 1848. It had 40in diameter wheels, and two cylinders $3\frac{1}{2}$in by 6in, and could reach 47mph.

In 1848 Adams built another larger vehicle called *Fairfield* to the designs of James Samuel, this time with six wheels, of which the driven pair were 54in diameter, and with cylinders 7in by 12in. This ran as No 29 on the Tiverton branch of the Bristol & Exeter Railway. *Fairfield* was followed during the next year by a larger 8-wheeled version named *Enfield*, which ran between Enfield and Angel Road, also on the Eastern Counties line. It had driving wheels 60in diameter with 8in by 12in cylinders, and once ran from London to Norwich (126 miles) in 3 hours 35 minutes. It was later converted to a 2–2–2 locomotive. Two further attempts in 1849 and in 1851, the latter by Kitsons of Leeds called *Ariel's Girdle* (which was shown at the Crystal Palace Exhibition) seem to have come to nothing. Apart from a couple of cars built by the Great Southern & Western Railway in Ireland in 1873, the railcar fades out until 1902. In 1902 Dugald Drummond of the London & South Western Railway revived the railcar era by building an 8-wheeled bogie car 56ft long with two cylinders 7in by 10in and a small vertical boiler operating at 150lb/sq

in. The wheels were 33in diameter, which reputedly gave a rather uncomfortable ride. This was built for the 1.2 mile branch from Fratton to East Southsea, which had been opened in 1885. Before going to its designated line, it was first tried out on the Great Western between Stroud and Chalford, a bit of line over which the Cheltenham Flyer was to work sometime later. This vehicle went into service on its own branch on 1 June 1903. It was followed by a second car, with two more for the Basingstoke to Alton line. The boiler of the first car proved inadequate and this was replaced in October 1903 by an ungainly horizontal version. The LSWR built nine more cars in 1905 and four in 1906.

The Great Western Railway really set the pace in the steam railcar business, building its first in 1903 following the trials of the LSWR version. By 1908 it had built 99 cars, mostly either $59\frac{1}{2}$ft or 70ft long. Fourteen were by Kerr Stuart and eight by the Gloucester Carriage & Wagon Company, but the rest were all Swindon-built, mostly with 12in by 16in cylinders and with 48in driving wheels, though the original one had 44in wheels. These cars were used all over the GWR system on routes later to be worked by the AEC railcars and later still by the underfloor DMUs. The steam cars lasted until 1917 when conversions began to driving trailers for use with auto-trains. Seventy-eight were converted and the rest were either sold or scrapped. Other lines following suit in 1903 were the Taff Vale and the Barry Railways.

Five more railways took to railcars in 1904 and in 1905 seventeen lines commissioned 67 cars (24 on the GWR alone) followed by 48 in 1906. Building then tailed off, with a finish in 1911 by three cars for the Lancashire & Yorkshire Railway. These steam cars had varied from 32 tons to $49\frac{1}{2}$ tons for a 66ft version for the Great Northern; most of the GWR 70ft versions weighed 43 tons.

Fairfield steam railcar, built by W. B. Adams in 1848.

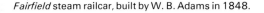

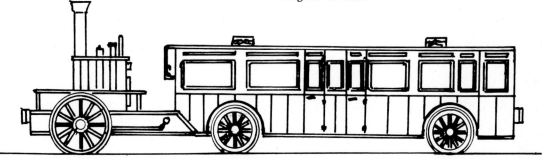

1849 steam railcar *Eagle*. (*BR/OPC*)

To complete the steam railcar story, mention should be made of some geared units built by the Sentinel-Cammell and the Clayton Wagon companies, starting in 1923. These were mostly used by the LNER, which purchased 74 in all. A few ran on the LMS and one on the Southern on the latter's Devil's Dyke branch from Brighton, but it was a last-ditch effort since the line closed on the 31 December 1938. This last vehicle had been supplied in 1933 at a cost of £2,680 and it had a 2-cylinder compound engine with $4\frac{1}{2}$in and $7\frac{1}{2}$in diameter cylinders by 6in stroke, giving 97hp with a steam pressure of 325lb/sq.in. The wheels were 30in

diameter with wooden centres and had internal expanding brakes. It suffered from fractured bogie bolsters and was sent eventually to the Westerham branch.

By contrast though, in 1905 the London, Brighton & South Coast Railway converted some Terrier 0–6–0 tanks for push-pull working, and this was followed by the NER and the GWR which used mainly 0–4–2 tank engines. From 1905 this version of the steam railcar was tried out in varying forms, either with a conventional small tank locomotive coupled to one or two coaches with a control cab at the outer end, or alternatively a similar locomotive permanently attached to a coach body or a complete coach with an inbuilt powered bogie. These variations were tried out by the Midland, the Great Central and the LNWR, which had over 60 variations in use all over its system by 1914.

LSWR steam railcar No 2, built in 1902 for use on the Fratton–Southsea branch. (*F. A. J. Emery-Wallis*)

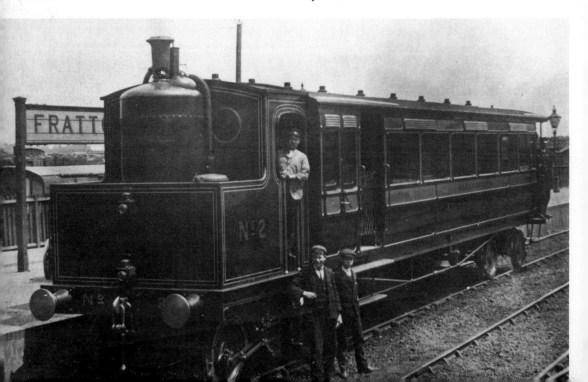

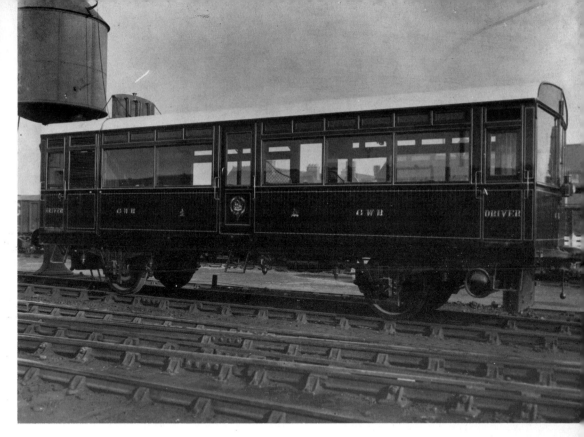

Great Western petrol-electric railcar built in 1912 and used experimentally on the Windsor branch. (*British Railways*)

The first Lancashire & Yorkshire Railway steam railcar with transverse boiler. (*London Midland Region, BR*)

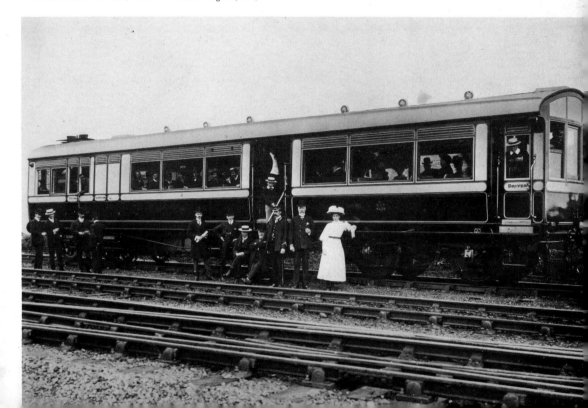

Power bogie of an LNWR railcar (*London Midland Region, BR*)

LNWR steam railcar No 1 (*London Midland Region, BR*)

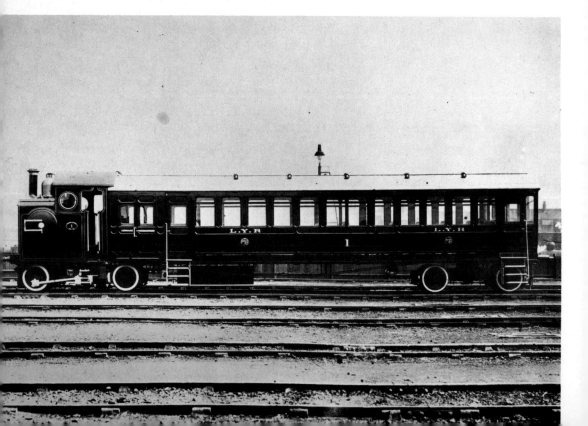

LNER Sentinel railcar No 248 *Tantivy* on the Midland & Great Northern line in 1933. (*Alan Whitehead*)

Diesel Railcars

During the time since the first railcars emerged some significant developments in the systems of motive power had taken place, starting with Lenoir's gas engine in 1860 and followed by Nikolaus Otto's 4-stroke engine, which ran on gas in 1862 and on liquid fuel in 1885. That year Gottlieb Daimler first put his high-speed (650rpm) gasoline engine into a road vehicle and in 1894 Rudolf Diesel got his compression ignition engine to run. In 1897 Diesel granted manufacturing licences to Sulzer in Switzerland, to Busch in the USA, to Carels in Belgium and to Mirrlees in Scotland. In 1894 an oil-engined vehicle built by Priestman Brothers had operated in the Alexandra Dock sidings at Hull, but being of only 30hp was really unable to perform any useful work.

Of greater impact to the main line and suburban steam railway networks was the development of rival electric traction systems in the form of underground railways and more particularly in the street tramcar; it was the Portsmouth trams that in 1903 caused the London & South Western Railway to build its first steam railcars.

In 1903 the North Eastern Railway was trying out a 4-cylinder petrol (gasoline)-electric car as was the Great Northern Railway, which had one built by Kerr Stuart with a Daimler engine. The LNWR had also commissioned in 1914 a 20-ton petrol-electric railcar built by the British Westinghouse Company with a body by Dick Kerr of Preston. The engine was by the Aster Engine Company of Wembley, giving 90hp at 1160rpm driving a 63kW generator and supplying two 64hp motors on one bogie. This was converted to a driving trailer in 1924 and finally written-off in 1941.

With growing competition from trams and motor buses, coupled with World War I (1914–18) followed by the amalgamation of 1923, little development in the diesel railcar took place in the United Kingdom until 1928.

Meanwhile, developments in Europe were more noticeable. In 1913 ASEA (which was to provide the power equipment for our first electric APT) in conjunction with Atlas produced a 75hp diesel railcar in Sweden at a cost of £3,490, followed by various sizes up to 300hp by 1925. In 1914 five 200hp Sulzer-engined diesel electric cars had been built for Prussia and Saxony, but again World War I affected developments. By the 1920s the use of the high-speed diesel engine resulting from the application of the Bosch direct injection fuel pump enabled railcar building in Germany, Denmark and Czechoslovakia with engines provided by Maybach, Daimler-Benz, Frichs and Tatra.

In 1928 the London Midland & Scottish Railway, from the advocacy of Alan Chorlton of Beardmore, produced a 500hp diesel-electric 4-car train set using a Beardmore engine similar to those designed for the airship R101, with electrics (by Dick Kerr then part of English Electric) built into one of the former power cars used on the LYR experimental 3,500v line from Bury to Holcombe Brook in Lancashire. This was the first DEMU in the UK, possibly anywhere. Although it was not a success either technically or operationally, it did lead to the English Electric Company becoming interested in diesel-electric traction and to the development of its own diesel engines for rail traction.

The Beardmore engine used in the LMS

11

The Great Western ran the largest fleet of steam railcars in Britain, built between 1903 and 1908. This is car No 61 with a trailer car. (*British Railways*)

experimental train was its 8-cylinder version with a bore of 8.25in and a stroke of 12in, running at 900rpm. In order to meet the weight requirements for airship work the engine scantlings were overstressed and trouble was experienced with crankcase fractures and big-end bearing failures, which were a common feature in the days of white metal bearings. Further, the engine bedplate was bolted solid to the coach underframe, so that distortions due to normal rail ride conditions had to be absorbed by the engine and the engine stresses transmitted to the underframe; this was before the 3-point suspension was generally adopted for power units. The engine had a steel crankcase and each cylinder head had four valves with aluminium covers. The governor selected the engine speed by electromagnets according to the controller position; the controller had seven positions giving the following sequence:

The first diesel-electric train in Europe: LMS 4-car unit, built 1928. (*GEC Traction*)

Armstrong Whitworth diesel-electric railcar *Northumbrian*. This was intended for the LMS and ran on that line as the Armstrong Shell Express. (*National Railway Museum*)

Position	
1 OFF	Engine idles at 350rpm.
2 Transition	Engine speed 600rpm. Circuit breaker closed.
3 1st Running notch	Generator shunt field circuit closed.
4 2nd Running notch	Engine speed 750rpm.
5 3rd Running notch	Engine speed 900rpm.
6 4th Running notch	First field divert.
7 5th Running notch	Second field divert.

The motor bogie was from Euston-Watford stock, probably a spare for the original LNWR Siemens trains, and was at the rear of the power car. Two

Michelin, the railcar built by the Michelin Tyre Co Ltd, as demonstrated on the LMS in 1932. (*National Railway Museum*)

275hp motors were fitted, supplied by the English Electric Company, which had taken-over the former Siemens works at Stafford.

Operation took place only on the level track between Preston and Blackpool and there is no record of any performance results, but one description mentions a speed of only 26mph in controller position 7. There is also no record of any heating method for the coaches, but this presumably came off the main generator and would have absorbed a good proportion of its output, which was only 340kW. With the demise of Beardmores shortly after the R101 disaster there was little spur to keep this unit operational, and it soon ceased to function.

Wm Beardmore also produced some railcars for Spain and Canada as well as supplying two of its 12-cylinder 12in bore engines rated at 1,300hp to the Canadian National Railway, which fitted them in a monstrous locomotive of 295 tons.

Following the Beardmore trials on the LMS, the

LMS 3-car diesel train, built at Derby in 1938. (*British Rail*)

next vehicle tried out was a device called the Ro-Railer. The LMS must be given full marks for trying out things, though as the largest commercial organisation in the UK (if not in the whole world at that time) with a capital of over £400 million it was perhaps its fate to be the testing ground. The Ro-Railer was a conventional bus shape, but had flanged steel wheels inboard of the normal rubber-tyred road wheels and could be arranged to run on either road or rail. The outer road wheels were mounted eccentrically to the rail wheels and could be lowered or raised to suit the mode of travel required. The rear road wheels were also geared to the rail wheels so that a top gear ratio of 4.2/1 was obtained on rail to give 75mph and the ratio on the road was 7/1; the changeover from road to rail or vice-versa could be completed in 2½ minutes. The chassis was provided by Karrier Motors Ltd of Huddersfield (now part of the Talbot Group) and the body was by the Cravens Railway Carriage & Wagon Company of Sheffield. A form of heating described as thermo-economic was employed, supplying heated air, using presumably the engine cooling system. The chassis was later fitted with standard height buffers and a drawhook to permit towing by a locomotive in the event of breakdown. Seating accommodation was for 26 passengers in a total weight of 7.1 tons. Petrol consumption was 8mpg on road and 16mpg on rail. It was first tried out on the branch line from Harpenden to Hemel Hempstead and later around Stratford-on-Avon. It was described as being supplied to the requirements of Mr. J. Shearman, Road Motor Engineer, so it is understandable that the CME was

not going to have any vehicle not under his control running around on rail. It soon disappeared from sight.

In 1932 the LMS tried out the rubber-tyred Michelin car, but before that there were three Sulzer engined railcars built by Armstrong Whitworth, intended for the LNER, the LMS and the Southern systems. These were fitted with Sulzer 6-cylinder engine type 6LV22 giving 250hp at 775rpm. The main generator was by Laurence Scott & Electromotors of Norwich, and there were two GEC traction motors. These cars had steel underframes and steel bodies provided by Cravens Ltd of Sheffield; the roof portion over the engine carried the radiators and could be removed to enable the power unit to be lifted out. Each car provided accommodation for 60 passengers. They were designed to pull trailers and to run as multiple units though there is only a record of their having done so once. The three cars were named *Tyneside Venturer*, *Northumbrian* and *Lady Hamilton*, the last being intended for the Southern Railway to coincide with its new 4–6–0 steam locomotive No E850 *Lord Nelson*. Though it made a run to Kings Cross in July 1932 it did not reach the Southern until April 1933, and then was reputed to have caught fire at New Cross. In 1934 it was back on the LNER working between Hull and Pontefract, putting up a weekly mileage of 2,300.

The *Tyneside Venturer* had given a demonstration run from Newcastle to Blackhill on 23 November 1931 to LNER officials including Nigel Gresley, and subsequently worked between York and Scarborough. It was purchased by the LNER in November 1932 for £7,500 and put to regular service around Scarborough.

The third car, *Northumbrian*, was sent to the LMS

carriage works at Wolverton and there refitted as a luxury saloon for 12 passengers, to provide a daily run in February and March 1933 between Euston and Castle Bromwich for the British Industries Fair. Renamed the *Armstrong Shell Express* it ran the 113 miles in 127 minutes and covered 2,420 miles in this service using 427 gallons of fuel, then costing 3.5d per gallon. It was subsequently reconverted to its original form and purchased by the LNER along with the *Lady Hamilton* for £5,500 each. During 1935 the three units averaged 51,300 miles per annum each for an overall cost including depreciation of 8.4d per mile. They continued in service until 1939 and were finally scrapped in 1944.

While the LNER was testing and finally adopting its three diesel-electric railcars, the LMS was providing the testing facilities for the rubber-tyred *Michelin* railcar. This was built in France and sponsored in the UK by the Michelin Tyre Company of Stoke-on-Trent, in whose publicity the following claims were made: that it could carry 24 passengers in a weight of 5 tons, cruise at 55mph with a petrol consumption of 12mpg, attain 50mph in 1000yd and stop from that speed in 110yd.

It was a 10-wheeled vehicle with a 27hp Panhard engine. The tyres were Michelin 910/125 inflated to 85lb/sq in, with a warning device that operated in the event of a loss of pressure of 14lb/sq in. The braking was by Lockheed hydraulic internal expanding brakes on all wheels. This vehicle operated between Bletchley and Oxford and on the occasion of a demonstration on the 16 February 1932 the following points were noted by the Author:–

A stopping run from Bletchley to Bicester was run in 30 minutes with seven stops against 42 minutes for the normal steam train timing, an average of 38.5mph. In an acceleration test between Bicester and Oxford 43mph was attained in 60 seconds and the return run non-stop from Oxford to Bletchley was run in 41 minutes, an average of 45.5mph. The riding was smooth and silent; in fact the latter was claimed as a disadvantage as it was inaudible to people working on the line. The cost of the car was given as £1,500 and one of the locations suggested for its use was on the Lancaster, Morecambe and Heysham line, as consideration was then being given to abandon the 6.6kV electric working on that line. There were a number of high-level operators from various overseas railways who saw these trials, but so far as is known no sales resulted. Some trials were also undertaken on the Southern around Alton in Hampshire and later on a more sophisticated version was tried out in the Cambridge area of the LNER.

In France a more conventional bus-shaped version based on a Hispona-Suiza chassis had run from Paris to the fashionable resort of Deauville at an average speed of 66mph (105kph), but still without any sales resulting, though maybe it had some influence on the later introduction of the rubber tyred stock on the Paris Metro.

The operating people had three specific objections which weighed against any further service operation which were (a) its inaudibility from the point of safety of lineside workers; (b) its inability to operate track circuits for signalling purposes; (c) its inability to haul a trailer to cope with extra traffic such as on market days (vital to many rural lines at that time) or to haul horse boxes which were also important traffic for many branch lines.

In 1932 was produced in Germany the most celebrated railcar of all time *Die Fliegende Hamburger*, a twin-car unit employing the new 12-cylinder Maybach diesel engine, running at 1,500rpm and giving 410hp. This train operated at an average speed of 77mph with a maximum of 103mph (165kph). The previous year a propeller-driven *Krukenburg* car had worked this route from Berlin to Hamburg at an *average* speed of 99.5mph, with a maximum of 124mph, but this was not considered suitable for everyday operation. The *Flying Hamburger* unit put the steam designers on their mettle and produced some noticeable speed increases in the UK and in France. This first train was soon followed in Germany by 13 more 2-car sets in 1935 with electric transmission, and by four 3-car sets in 1936, two with electric and two with hydraulic transmission. These latter trains had the turbocharged version of the Maybach GO engine, giving 600hp.

By 1932 there were some 700 railcars of various types operating in the USA, mostly employing gasoline-electric power units with outputs up to 400hp, with sometimes two power units to a coach. One particular USA engine, the Winton 194–12, designed to run on low-grade gasoline or distillate, had been developed to give 900hp at 900rpm. This engine was to provide the basis for the General Motors EMD range of locomotive diesel engines, first the 201A models used in the *City of Portland* and *Burlington Zephyr* and later 567 and 645 versions, the latter still being in production.

With the demise of Beardmore in 1931 some of its diesel team went to the English Electric Diesel Division and there produced two new engines. The first was a 10in bore by 12in stroke model K, a 6-cylinder version of which was first used in shunting or switching locomotives and which became the standard BR 6KT engine still in use in the Class 08 and Class 09 units. The other was an 8in by 10in engine known as the H model. This H engine, which ran at up to 1,500rpm, was very similar to the Beardmore but with a cast-iron crankcase, and was only produced in a 6-cylinder form; for rail traction it was known as the 6HT.

In order to obtain trials and proving experience English Electric built at its Preston works a railcar called *Bluebird*, employing one of these engines rated at 200hp. This car was tried out on the LMS, and as the engine had been built at Rugby this was first used on the line between Rugby and Market Harborough, later being transferred to work from Bletchley to

Bedford. The underframe was built to full railway standards and was designed to haul a trailer, but the power was quite inadequate for this duty and it seems to have just faded away. The experience seems to have been worthwhile, since similar engines were later supplied in railcars for Ceylon and Western Australia.

The engine had suffered from big-end bearings failures and from heavy camshaft wear, and similar failures were experienced in Ceylon. Unfortunately the amount of running in the UK was not sufficient to permit a solution to these problems, and they had to be met and overcome in a country a long way from home, which is always a much more expensive exercise.

In the same year as *Bluebird* was being tried out on the LMS the first of the AEC railcars appeared on the Great Western Railway, and they will be considered in the next chapter.

The last of the pre-World War II (1939/45) railcars other than the AEC models was a beautiful 3-car train liveried in red and aluminium built by the LMS at Derby in 1938 with articulated bogies and streamlined nose ends.

Each car was fitted with two 125hp Leyland engines driving through a Leyland Lysholm Smith torque converter transmission to the nearest axle on each bogie. Since the set was articulated all axles were driving axles except the outer one on each end bogie. The engines were mounted vertically on the centre line of the coach between the main frames and were extremely difficult to reach for maintenance purposes. The radiators were also mounted vertically between the frames without mechanical fans and relied on air scoops to supply the cooling air according to the direction of motion. This arrangement probably caused overheating problems and was never repeated on any subsequent railcars. The drive from the torque converters was taken by cardan shaft to a reversing gearbox mounted on the driving axles, the reversing selection being actuated by compressed air which also worked the engine controls and the vehicle brakes. The full air pressure was maintained at 105lb/sq in by means of six compressors, three engine-driven (one to each car) one on the centre car driven off the transmission, and two electrically-driven. The pressure in the control system was reduced to 15lb/sq in.

All wheels were braked by Ferodo composition brake shoes worked off a 5in diameter cylinder for each wheel.

The controls were actuated by electro-pneumatic valves worked off a 24v system, which also provided the coach lighting and the engine starter motors. There were six batteries, four at 390amp-hours and two at 210amp-hours; they were supplied by two Stone's Tonum 125-amp generators on engines 1 and 6 as well as one bus type generator driven off the propellor shaft in the centre car.

The underframes were welded and carried on two longitudinal trusses, the whole being mounted on four bogies; the centre two were of a type not previously used in the UK. A horizontal link 15ft long was pivoted on the bogie centre and at the ends to the underframes, but the body weight was taken by rollers on the bogie bolster. The bogies were also fabricated, using high-tensile steel, and the axleboxes were fitted with SKF roller bearings. The wheels were 3ft 0in diameter, mounted on hollow axles.

The bodies were built of teak pillars with steel bracing. The roof sheets and bodyside panels were welded before being secured to the timber framework. The inside surfaces were all sprayed with asbestos $\frac{1}{4}$in thick, increased in the area of the power units. The sliding doors were air-operated and could be worked by guard or passengers. Heating was by steam supplied at 30lb/sq in from a Clarkson waste heat boiler mounted between the two engines and fed by the exhaust gasses from both engines. The exhaust then passed vertically through the lavatory compartment to a fishtail outlet on the roof. The body interiors were panelled in 3-ply veneer; the woods used included West African cherry mahogany and Pacific quilted maple. The lighting (which was rather crude) consisted of roof-mounted open bulbs. Roof torpedo ventilators extracted both from the passenger space and from the air spaces between the inner and outer skins, so as to reduce condensation. There was provision for 162 seats of which 24 were first-class, and the total weight was 73 tons.

The set first operated between Cambridge and Oxford in an attempt to provide a good service between these two university cities. The normal steam-operated service then usually involved a change at either Bedford or Bletchley, while the one through train in the day took $2\frac{1}{4}$ hours for the 77 miles. It could easily be motored in that time, and some enthusiasts with Bentleys or Bugattis claimed to have done it in under even time. The diesel set did the journey in 105 minutes with stops at Sandy, Bedford and Bletchley, but when it was out of commission – a fairly frequent occurrence – the service was provided by a 2–6–4 tank hauling two corridor coaches. In order to keep time speeds of over 80mph were needed in places, and since the locomotive did not have much in hand it had to be worked fairly hard.

Since the Oxford to Cambridge service resulted in no increase in revenue, in spite of clamours for a better service, this set was later used between St Pancras and Bedford with occasional runs to Nottingham, but it was not suited to main line duties having no buffet facilities and like so many LMS ventures it just died from lack of knowing what to do with it.

The whole unit was well conceived in spite of some shortcomings, and if the 1939 war had not intervened it might have proved the forerunner of a number of railcar sets. It worked until early in 1940 when it was withdrawn and later converted into an electrification maintenance unit.

2 The AEC Railcars

The first successful fleet application of diesel railcars in the UK was made by the Great Western Railway, using the standard AEC Hardy bus engine in conjunction with a transmission system consisting of a Vulcan Sinclair fluid flywheel and a Wilson preselector epicyclic gearbox as used in Daimler motor cars. Starting with a design drawn up in December 1932, these railcars eventually amounted to 38 power cars, the last two being delivered in February 1942 and remaining in service until 1962.

The Great Western had tried out a petrol-electric railcar in 1911 embodying a 40hp Maudslay engine with BTH electrics, and had run this on the Windsor branch until 1919 when it was sold to Lever Brothers at Port Sunlight. The experience with this vehicle resulted in the GWR waiting until a suitable diesel engine was available. It was offered to the Great Western by the AEC Equipment Company of Southall in the form of a standard Regal bus fitted with flanged wheels, which was tried out between Southall and Brentford. The problems involved in turning this vehicle at each end of the journeys led to the design of a 70-seat double-ended vehicle produced by the Hardy Rail Car Company, a subsidiary of AEC which had started itself as a subsidiary of the London General Omnibus Company to maintain and later to produce vehicles and engines for the London bus services.

The first cars, which were of a streamlined form, were designed by Mr C. F. Cleaver of AEC to the requirements of Mr C. B. Collett, Chief Mechanical Engineer of the GWR. It employed an AEC 6-cylinder diesel engine 115mm bore by 142mm stroke, rated nominally at 130hp but designed for this duty to give 121hp at 2,000rpm. This engine employed a Ricardo pre-combustion chamber in the cylinder head, since this was found necessary to ensure good combustion and to eliminate diesel knock at the idling speed, which was 450rpm. By 1933 some 3,000 of these engines had been produced and these had achieved over 10 million miles of operation on the highway, but there are differences in operation when on a railborne chassis which affected the performance of engines and other equipment.

The streamlined ends of the No 1 railcar were evolved as a result of wind tunnel tests at the AEC works. The design was stated to have been a mixture of the Krukenburg propeller-driven railcar which had achieved 124mph and the dickey seat of an early Morris Oxford 2-seater motor car.

The engine was mounted vertically on the outside of the main frame, with the radiator at the free end as in a commercial vehicle and cooled by a fan mounted on the engine casing. In order to provide adequate air flow to the radiator when travelling with the radiator behind the engine a hinged flap was fitted to deflect air passing under the car bodywork onto the radiator grille.

The power output from the fluid flywheel was taken by cardan shaft to a 4-speed Wilson epicyclic gearbox and then by another shaft to the reversing gearbox. From there a further cardan shaft went to the first worm drive axlebox and finally to the other axle of the driven bogie, making four cardan shafts in all.

The car body, built by the Park Royal Coachworks, was of aluminium sheets on an oak framework, with the side panels down to within 10in of rail level. It was built as an open vestibule type with central doors, a driver's compartment at one end and a driver's luggage compartment at the other. There was provision for 69 seated third-class passengers.

The brakes were of the automotive type, internal expanding with Ferodo-lined shoes acting on 20in diameter cast-steel drums bolted to the inside of one wheel on each axle. The master cylinder was a Lockheed hydraulic type operated by a Clayton-Dewandre vacuum cylinder. Clayton-Dewandre heaters were installed in the passenger saloon to provide heat supplied by the engine cooling system.

No 1 was put into service in the Reading Area on 4 December 1933, but was soon withdrawn for modifications to the braking system. It was then fitted with automatic train control apparatus and returned to duty on 5 February 1934. Its initial operation was from Southall to Slough, Windsor, Reading and Didcot. As a result of its success three further cars were commissioned during 1934, but they were of a high-speed type with buffet. They had two engines, each giving a maximum speed of 80mph, for use on an express service between Birmingham and Cardiff. In these cars 44 seats were provided, 40 in two saloons with fixed tables and four in the buffet section. Two toilets were also provided. The interior decoration was by Heal & Son, the exclusive furnishing firm of Tottenham Court Road, London. These cars were fitted with automatic train control from the outset, and had special buffers and concealed drawgear for use in emergency.

On these first twin-engined cars the radiators were placed in a similar position to that on No 1, but made

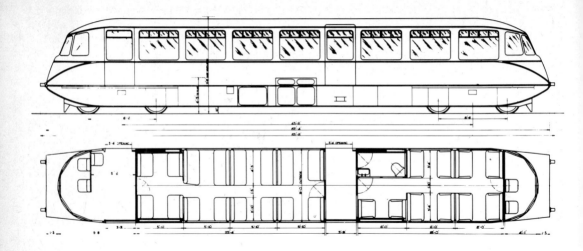

Diagram of AEC railcar No 1, built by Park Royal in 1933
for the GWR. (*G. Passey*)

Interior view of AEC express buffet railcar, as used on the
GWR Birmingham—Swansea service. (*G. Passey*)

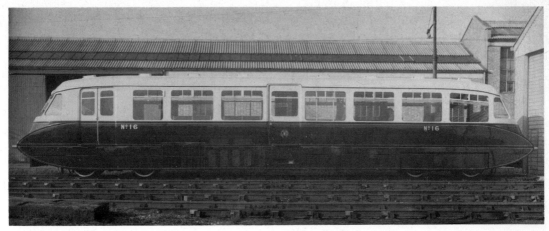

Twin-engine AEC railcar No 16, built by Gloucester Railway Carriage & Wagon Co. (*G. Passey*)

wider and placed at 45 degrees, with a deflecting chamber and a hinged flap also with louvres at 45 degrees pointing in both directions. The second engine did not drive through a gearbox, but direct to the reversing box. A compensating device was fitted so that full output could only be obtained from the second power unit when top gear had been selected on the other gearbox driven by the first engine. The second power unit only drove on one axle of its driving bogie. This was later to be a common feature. The bodies of cars Nos 2 to 4 were built by the Gloucester Carriage & Wagon Company, owing to pressure of work at Park Royal.

During 1935 a further three cars, Nos 5 to 7, were

Parcels car No 17 at Southall. (*G. Passey*)

built. They were of the suburban traffic type with 70 seats, mechanics similar to Nos 2–4 and bodies by Gloucester C. & W. Company. They were followed in 1936 by a further ten cars the last of which, No 17, was a parcels car for use between Southall and Oxford; this was intended to reduce loading times at stations for ordinary passenger trains. On these cars, Nos 8 to 17, a gearbox was introduced into the line from the second engine, since this had been tried put in car No 7 and found (not un-naturally) to improve acceleration. The drive was also taken to all four axles.

No 18 produced in 1937 was a radical departure from the previous types since this was intended for use on the Lambourn branch from Newbury, and it was essential for it to be able to pull horseboxes. The chassis was considerably stronger and was fitted with standard buffers and drawgear capable of accepting up to 60 tons (two standard coaches or eight horseboxes). Seating accommodation was reduced to 49, but extra luggage space was provided. The controls were electro-

Chassis for AEC railcar No 18, designed to haul a trailing load -- originally intended for the Lambourn branch. (*G. Passey*)

pneumatic for operation from trailer cars fitted with driver's controls, and for multiple-unit operation with other similarly equipped cars.

The reversing gearbox was eliminated by the use of reversing dogs in the axle drive box. As a result of shortening the transmission system the two engines could be mounted opposite each other on a rubber-suspended subframe at the centre of the chassis. The empty weight of the complete vehicle had gone up from 24 tons for No 1 to 33.6 tons in the case of No 18, which was 2ft 0in longer at 65ft 8in.

Car No 18 was the last to be supplied by an outside contractor and the remaining twenty were all built at Swindon, ten in 1940, eight in 1941, and the last two in February 1942. The basic chassis design was as for No 18, and in these the change in position of the engines allowed the radiators to be placed at right-angles to the engine and so use a larger fan of 32in diameter instead of 26in as before. The fan drive was by bevel gears and a belt; the larger fan running at a lower speed saved 25 percent of the power loss for that drive.

On the last twenty cars the transmission was similar to that tried out on No 18 and consisted of a 5-speed epicyclic gear box having ratios of 1/1, 1.64/1, 2.53/1, 4.5/1 and 6.38/1 (the latter for emergency use only on steep gradients). At the output end of this gearbox was a further dual-ratio reduction box having five alternative ratios, 1.03/1, 1.15/1, 1.37/1, 1.73/1 and 1.96/1; this box could be arranged so that any two of these ratios were available for the driver's selection, thus giving a choice of top speeds between 75mph and 40mph with maximum tractive efforts from 4,360lb to 8,340lb.

On No 18 the pneumatic gear selector relied on a set of calibrated springs and variable air pressures between 10lb/sq in and 80lb/sq in to obtain the various gear ratios. This was not satisfactory for multiple-unit working and on the other cars an air motor was used which contained three pistons. By selection of various ports, five distinct movements were possible at any air pressure between 40lb/sq in and 80lb/sq in. On Nos 19 to 38 the cylinder diameter of the AEC diesel engine was increased to 120mm, with a direct injection cylinder head, and the output was adjusted to 105hp at 1,650rpm. The engines were re-positioned further from the bogies they drove so that the radiators were central and opposite each other with the drive shaft passing behind the radiator framework. The main chassis frames were stronger and wider, while the nose end of the bodywork was squared-off to give more floor space.

The bogie wheelbase had been increased to 8ft 6in on No 18 and was the same on the remaining twenty; the leaf springs had also been increased to 4ft 8in, which gave improved ride qualities. Standard railway type clasp brakes were also adopted, vacuum-operated by 18in cylinders. Four rotary exhausters were employed, two for each power system. Two air compressors with 9 cu ft/min capacity provided air at 80 lb/sq in for controls, sanding and the Desilux air horns (two pairs at each end) which were audible $3\frac{1}{2}$ miles away.

The last four cars, Nos 35 to 38, were arranged to operate in pairs with a trailer coach in between and each had only one driving compartment. These were the heaviest units of the lot with weights of 36.7 tons for Nos 35 and 37 and 37.6 tons for Nos 36 and 38. No 34 was a parcels van with a weight of 34.9 tons and a capacity of 10 tons, similar to that for No 17.

As previously noted, No 1 commenced operations between Southall and Reading in February 1934 and in July the next two units initiated a limited-stop buffet car service between Birmingham and Cardiff, covering the 116.8 miles in 142 minutes with stops at Gloucester

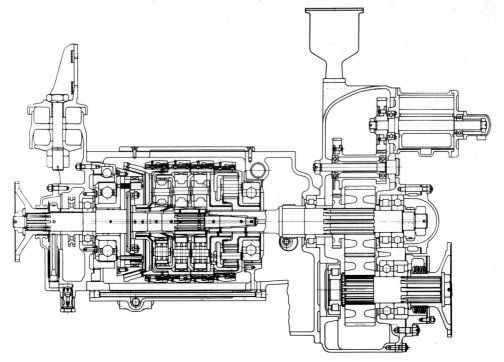

Arrangement of Wilson 5-speed gearbox. (*G. Passey*)

and Newport, an average speed of 49.3mph. Before going into service a press run was made on 3 July from Paddington to Oxford and back in which 44 miles were run in 40 minutes. This was followed on 4 July by a run from Paddington to Birmingham, when a maximum speed of 76mph was attained near Princess Risborough. The first two cars each ran one round trip a day and in September they were joined by the third unit so that there was always one spare car to cover servicing arrangements and possible breakdowns.

In July 1935 three of the 70-seaters started work, one at Oxford and two at Worcester, followed by a further ten in 1936. With four spare cars, one buffet car at Birmingham and the other three at Bristol, Newport and Worcester, the depot allocation and daily mileage for the 1936 summer service was as follows:

Depot	No of cars	Daily mileage
Southall	1	238
Oxford	2	551
Bristol	1	356
Weymouth	1	282
Cheltenham	1	272
Pontypool	1	240

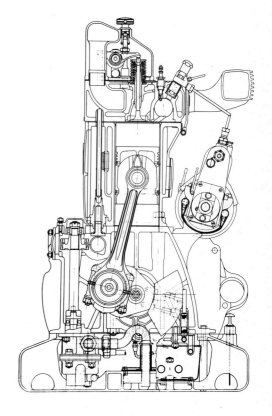

Cross-section diagram of AEC 6-cylinder diesel engine. (*G. Passey*)

AEC dry sump diesel engine. (*G. Passey*)

Worcester	2	514
Birmingham	1	305
Cardiff	1	286
Swansea	1	229

The daily mileage of 3,273 represented three percent of the total daily passenger mileage on the GWR. The total annual mileage for these seventeen cars was just over one million, while No 1 had achieved over 150,000 miles in three years of operation. There were thirteen runs at over 50mph, and the fastest was run by the Weymouth car from Castle Cary to Westbury in 18 minutes at 65.8mph – no hanging about on the main line. The longest non-stop daily run was between Birmingham and Cheltenham, a distance of 54 miles which was run in 61 minutes.

By April 1937 No 18 was in service and some timed runs were made between Brentford and Southall with

Preserved GWR railcars Nos 4 and 22, contrasting the two designs. (*R. H. G. Simpson*)

up to four trailer cars or 124 tons. The 3.3 miles were run start-to-stop as follows:

No of trailers	Time (minutes)
Nil	5.3
1	6.2
2	7.1
3	8.3
4	10.7

Mr C. F. Cleaver of AEC summed up progress and lessons learned, in a paper to the GWR Swindon Engineering Society in November 1937. Car No 1 had run nearly 200,000 miles and the total fleet mileage was then almost two million miles. The oil cooling on the engines had not at first proved adequate and a water-cooled grid was laid in the crankcase sump through which the hot oil had to pass. This increased the engine weight from 1,414lb to just under 1,500lb. On No 18 the engine was of the dry sump type which allowed a reduction in the engine height so that the raised portions of the floor over the older type engines could be dispensed with.

The self-changing Wilson epicyclic gearbox relied on

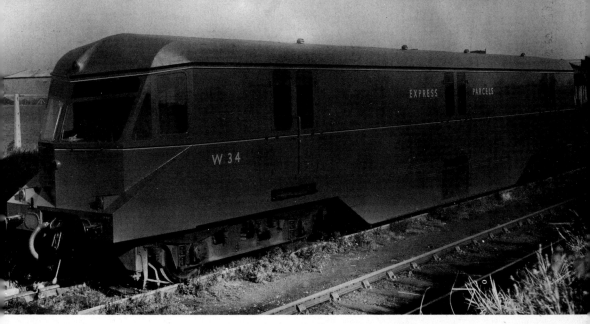

Parcels van No 34 in BR all-over crimson lake livery, shortly after nationalisation of the railways in 1948. (*G. Passey*)

friction bands to hold the outer wheel of the engaged gear, and in order to allow for wear in these bands they were fitted with a self-adjusting screw which should automatically take up every time the selector was operated. On these boxes the operation was too slow to actuate this device and stronger springs had to be fitted.

On the first of the reverse gearboxes straight teeth were used and these proved very noisy in service; double helical teeth were then employed, but even these were not satisfactory until the teeth were ground. The first driving axle gearboxes were of the worm drive type, but the bellows glands were prone to fail, which resulted in some ruined gears due to loss of oil. These were supplemented with a felt washer which, though not perfect, did allow a much longer life. On No 18 a

Early days of nationalisation: GWR railcar No W20W in British Railways carmine-and-cream express passenger livery. (*R. H. G. Simpson*)

bevel drive was used which allowed a reversing device to be incorporated, using a sliding dog clutch which could be remotely controlled by compressed air.

On the first seven cars plain bearing universal joints were used on the cardan shafts, but on the next ten cars they were superseded by the more up-to-date needle roller type, which had been found quite satisfactory on road vehicles. This type, however, would not stand up to railway application and after 50,000 miles they had to be replaced by the original plain bearing type.

The first seventeen cars had bogies with a 7ft 0in wheelbase and the side bearing leaf springs were 3ft 0in long on the first seven cars and 4ft 0in long on the other ten. On car No 18 the bogie wheelbase was increased to 8ft 6in and the springs to 4ft 8in long, with a considerable improvement in the riding qualities. In order to reduce the side sway on single cars at high speed on the Birmingham to Cardiff service it was found necessary to fit a bus type hydraulic shock absorber to the solebars and to connect them to the spring bolster, which also improved the ride.

Just before Nos 35 and 36 were put into service some trials were conducted between May 1940 and October

Another view of GWR railcar No 22, as British Railways No W22W, and in all-over BR green livery, with early style warning 'V' on front. (*R. H. G. Simpson*)

1941 with various combinations of cars and trailers in both high and low gear ratios with the results shown in Table 4. The maximum recorded speed during these tests was 68mph. The time taken to do all this was no doubt the result of wartime operation since the tests coincided with the Dunkirk evacuation and the Battle of Britain.

During 1944 Nos 6 and 19 were on loan to the LNER. The first car to be withdrawn was No 9 in May 1946 had been burnt out at Heyford in July 1945. By then the Birmingham buffet cars could not cope with the traffic that they had initiated, and had been diverted to work between Bristol and Reading. The allocation of the 37 cars in service in 1947 was as follows:– Southall 2, Reading 5, Oxford 2, Bristol 4, Weymouth 1, Leamington 2, Stourbridge 3, Gloucester 1, Worcester 7, Newport 2, Llantrisant 2, Pontypool 1, Camarthen 2, Landore 3.

Further losses occurred when No 37 was in a fire in 1947, and when No 2 was involved in a collision in 1953, leaving an allocation in 1955 of 35 cars as follows:– Southall 5, Reading 4, Oxford 4, Bristol 5, Weymouth 1, Leamington 3, Stourbridge 3, Worcester 6, Gloucester 1, Newport 2, Landore 1.

With the coming of nationalisation the cars were repainted in the standard crimson lake and cream, except for parcels cars Nos 17 and 34 which were all-over crimson. With the advent of the new underfloor railcars commencing with Classes 116 and 120 in 1957 the AEC fleet was down to 13 cars by 1962, and all were withdrawn by the end of that year.

Three remain in being: No 4 preserved at Didcot, No 20 on the Kent & East Sussex and No 22 at Bridgnorth on the Severn Valley Railway, preserved by the Great Western Society. No 20 had an interesting journey to Robertsbridge as it had to be loaded with brake blocks on one side to tilt the body to permit passage through the restricted tunnels at Tunbridge Wells, Wadhurst and Mountfield on its last run on BR metals in 1965.

RAILCAR TRIALS SOUTHALL–WESTBURY **MAY 1940–OCTOBER 1941**

Test No.		1	2	3	4	5	6	7
Formation		Car only	Car only	Car and one trailer	Car and one trailer	Car and two trailers	Car and two trailers	Two cars and one trailer
Weight, tons		35.6	35.6	68.9	68.9	102.2	102.2	108
Ratio		Low	High	Low	High	Low	High	
Intermediate mileages and start to stop speeds:	*Miles*	*mph*	*mph*	*mph*	*mph*	*mph*	*mph*	*mph*
Southall–Slough	$9\frac{1}{2}$	35.8	49.5	38.6	38.0	33.5	36.2	(B)
Slough–Reading	$17\frac{1}{2}$	43.8	56.1	39.0	42.8	35.0	36.8	43.5
Reading–Newbury	17	35.2	49.8	38.8	38.4	32.4	35.2	45.0
Newbury–Bedwyn	$13\frac{1}{2}$	42.0	50.5	39.6	39.6	33.7	34.4	42.5
Bedwyn–Patney	$14\frac{1}{2}$	41.5	48.3	38.7	43.5	32.8	37.4	44.5
Patney–Westbury	$14\frac{1}{2}$	42.9	52.7	41.5	45.8	38.6	42.5	27.0 (C)
Average speed–Down trip	$86\frac{1}{2}$	40.0	51.3	39.2	41.2	34.2	36.9	41.0
Westbury–Southall–Up trip	$86\frac{1}{2}$	38.6 (A)	54.9	42.6	45.1	38.9	39.6	52.0
Average–both trips	173	38.4	53.0	41.0	43.0	36.4	38.3	46.5
Fuel consumption, mpg		7.0	6.6	5.23	5.85	4.95	4.86	3.6 (D)
Ton-miles per gallon		249.0	235.0	360.0	403.0	505.0	497.0	396.0
Comparison, ton mpg x mph		1.0	1.36	1.55	1.81	1.93	1.98	1.93

(A) Includes three checks of $13\frac{1}{2}$ minutes. (B) Stop at Slough omitted; (C) Includes $12\frac{1}{2}$-minute stop outside Westbury: ignoring this figure raises average speed for both trips to 48.3mph; (D) For two cars, ie, 7.2mpg per car.

3 The British Railways DMU stock

On Vesting Day, 1 January 1948 when the railways of Great Britain were nationalised, the diesel railcar stock stood at 37 vehicles, 35 of the former Great Western Railway AEC type and two of the former LNER, built by Armstrong Whitworth. Since the foremost necessity at that time was the replacement of the ravages of the 1939/45 war by new stock, the accent was on the building of steam locomotives and standard passenger and freight rolling stock. There was also an acute shortage of oil fuel so there was little inclination toward the building of any types of diesel-propelled vehicles.

The first move toward the diesel railcar was the appointment of a committee (everything was done by committee in those days) under the terms of Railway Executive Memorandum M4051 of 9 August 1951 *To Consider and Report on the Scope for the Employment of Lightweight Trains*. This Committee under the chairmanship of H. G. Bowles of the Western Region produced a favourable report in 1952 which recommended the building and trial of some lightweight diesel multiple units. This was the result of a review of railcar operation in Europe where over 3,000 such cars were in service, particularly in France (720), Germany (850) and Belgium (110) and schemes were proposed for operation primarily in three areas, Lincolnshire, Leeds and West Cumberland. Operating costs per mile were estimated to be 28d ($11\frac{1}{2}$p) for a 2-car set and 41d (17p) for a 3-car or 4-car set, against 66d ($27\frac{1}{2}$p) to 86d (36p) for equivalent steam trains then in operation on those services.

The Lincolnshire scheme was estimated to cost £325,000 and to save £121,000 per annum. The Leeds area scheme was estimated at £200,000 with economies of £25,000 and extra traffic at £31,000 per annum. The West Cumberland scheme, which embraced Carlisle to Silloth, Whitehaven and Newcastle was down for £915,000, with a benefit of £133,000 per annum.

Other schemes suggested included from Edinburgh to Carlisle (the Waverley Route), Edinburgh to Glasgow and to North Berwick, with also 24 sets for the Bristol area and thirteen 2-car diesel-electric sets for the Hampshire area of the Southern Region.

The report also mentioned that in Germany plans were being submitted to build 3-car sets with two 1,000hp engines and 4-car sets with two 1,200hp engines for high-speed international services. The report was backed up with a memorandum by R. C. Bond, Member for Mechanical Engineering, to the Railways Board recommending the use of diesel railcars on the 168 routes then being worked by push-pull steam trains.

With the end of fuel rationing the climate for oil fuel was more favourable, and in November 1952 the first order was placed on Derby works to produce eight 2-car sets for the West Riding area of Yorkshire costing £275,000 and for thirteen 2-car sets for West Cumberland, at a cost of £332,000. Allowing for spares this put the cost of a power car at around £16,000 and a trailer at £7,500.

The first sixteen power cars (motor brake second Nos E79000 to E79007 and motor composite Nos E79500 to E79507) were fitted with two Leyland 6-cylinder horizontal type 125hp engines which drove through a Leyland Lysholm Smith torque converter as used on the pre-war LMS 3-car diesel set. These torque converters, which consisted of a double-acting clutch driving either through the converter or direct to the output shaft, hydraulically selected and with a free wheel to allow for overrun in either drive, were the last of this type of transmission produced by Leyland, since its road vehicle side had decided to concentrate on the pre-selector system and without quantity production the Lysholm Smith converter became uncompetitive. The drive from each converter was to the inner axle of each bogie through bevel gears which incorporated the reversing dogs. The final drive gearing, with a ratio of 3.58/1, was designed for a top speed of 62mph.

The bodies of these lightweight cars were built of ICI Kynal M39/2 Alloy using specially designed extrusions for the underframe, coachwork and floor members with cladding sheets of the same material; the inside structure and floor were insulated by sprayed asbestos. The brakes were of the vacuum type by Gresham & Craven to the quick release system. The heating was by Smith's oil-fired combustion type heaters supplying warm air through ducting at floor level.

The bogies were of a BR standard design in mild steel with sprung side-controlled bolsters and equipped with Timken roller-bearing axleboxes.

The driver's controls consisted of engine speed, clutch and direction as well as the usual braking and deadman's device. There were four engine speed positions and the clutch control also gave four selections; Off, Neutral, Converter Drive and Direct Drive.

Using two LMS 1926 all-steel Open Brake Seconds, Derby built this 2-car diesel electric set, which incorporated Paxman ZHXL 450hp under-floor engines. (*GEC Diesels Ltd/Paxman Diesels*)

The body interior was of the open saloon type and was finished in flameproof hardboard covered in pvc cloth. The seats had tubular steel frames finished in moquette. Good visibility was provided by ample window space, the passengers at the driving ends having a view of the track ahead, which was a novel attraction. The completed weight was 26 tons for the motor brake second and 27 tons for the motor composite.

In the production of these railcars, which was carried out in the Carriage & Wagon Works at Derby, the C&W Department handled this project on its own without seeking any advice from the Mechanical Engineering side, and this accounted for some of the early problems which were largely due to poor pipework and wiring. In the connecting sockets at the coach ends all three pins were of the same size so that they could be wrongly connected if joined by unskilled staff.

The first of these railcar sets came out of the works several months late and was then demonstrated at

Paxman/BTH generator set used in under-floor engine railcar No 9828. (*GEC Traction*)

Marylebone on 29 April 1954, with a trial run to Beaconsfield and back.

Before going into service in Yorkshire a further demonstration run was made from Leeds to Harrogate with a 2-car set for the benefit of the Press, and with the Area General Manager aboard. Soon after leaving Leeds one engine of the four cut out to be followed by a further one just before Harrogate. A quick check there showed that the pipes conveying the coolant for the torque converters had become loose and that all the fluid had been lost from the two failed power units. The remaining joints were then secured as far as possible in the time available, and though a further transmission failed on the return journey it was safely completed on the one remaining unit, much to the relief of the General Manager. Some speedy action was then taken to provide proper pipe joints before the service was inaugurated.

Two further problems arose in connection with this West Riding project, the training of drivers and maintenance staff, plus the fact that no suitable premises had been made available for the stabling and maintenance of the sets before their arrival from Derby. The driver problem was the one encountered all over the railway during the modernisation scheme – the most senior drivers were allocated to the new units because they were expected to put in the best mileage and so secure the best payments, whereas on the continent of Europe the drivers chosen were those with

the best learning aptitudes. In the UK they were the least adaptable and amenable to learning the new skills, which had to cope with electrical and automotive type faults rather than with the steam techniques that they were used to; this was eventually overcome, but results might have been better had the European system been adopted.

For this Yorkshire scheme the old Great Northern motive power depot at Bradford was allocated for the maintenance of the units. It was quite unsuitable for access to the underfloor equipment and as its interior had been whitewashed continually since about 1850, it was always shedding flakes of whitewash onto any work in hand at floor level. There was no suitable clean room for the servicing of the fuel injection equipment and other delicate components comparatively new to railway operation.

These lessons were learned the hard way, as is often the case with an inaugural scheme, and fortunately were more widely applied by the time the main line diesel locomotives began to come into service. It might be mentioned that the first really up-to-date diesel maintenance depot in the UK was that provided by the Steel Company of Wales in 1954 for its diesel locomotive fleet, then the largest privately-operated one in the country.

By the time that the West Riding service was started up the railcar programme had been increased to include 27 units for East Anglia and Lincolnshire as well as for further sets for the Newcastle area and for the Scottish Region, the total budget for which came to £2,000,000 (Barely the cost of a couple of trains nowadays.)

The service was introduced on 14 June 1954 between Leeds and Bradford, being an immediate success from the point of view of traffic. Even this was not sufficient to justify the cost of the new stock and ten years later the service was withdrawn, despite an increase in receipts of up to 400 percent in seven years.

The second batch of 13 sets was destined for the West Cumberland area and consisted of 2-car units with one power car pet set, this time fitted with two AEC 150hp diesel engines driving through a fluid flywheel and a Wilson 4-speed epicyclic preslector gearbox as used on the former GWR railcars. The units were put into service late in 1954 and immediately ran into problems due to an intense cold spell. It had not been intended to use anti-freeze in these engines initially because of its effect on rubber hoses and the costs of replenishment; engines had to be kept running for days on end, but eventually a glycol mixture with a phosphate-based inhibitor was allowed to be used without any ill effects, at least on the engines. On these units the driving trailer weighed 21 tons so that each 2-car set came to only 48 tons for a total of 123 seats. The introduction of these railcars was an instant success and increased traffic by 40 percent in nine months.

While these first two schemes were being implemented, the structure of British Railways was re-organised and the Modernisation Plan was being prepared including a three-year construction programme for up to 4,600 diesel railcars. Two vehicle lengths were planned, the shorter version at 57ft 0in for the London Midland Region and the North Eastern Region (by reason of clearance restrictions) and a longer version at 63ft 6in for the Eastern, Western and Scottish Regions. Whether in reality the longer coaches could not have run on LM and NE services is another matter; the length of 57ft was fairly standard on the LM and it was probably a restriction of the mind because that was what had always applied before. It was doubtful if anyone had actually checked clearances to see whether longer vehicles could be accommodated.

A review of all the carriage building capacity in the UK, both of the railway workshops and those or private industry led to large orders being placed during 1954 for these varying types of railcar for various duties. Those vehicles produced by the private sector will be considered in the next chapter, starting with some 4-wheel cars that had been built by the British United Traction Company in 1952. That concern had been formed to act as a co-ordinating outlet for sales and design of engines produced by the Leyland and AEC firms, as well as the associated transmission and control equipment to provide a complete power installation for railcars.

The first of the longer bodied cars were produced from the Swindon Works for the Scottish Region, using AEC 150hp engines. Before they came out, Derby produced some further lightweight sets for both Eastern and London Midland Regions. They were for services in Lincolnshire and in East Anglia as well as for the Birmingham to Swansea and the Watford to St Alban's branch, the latter being a first venture for DMU sets in the London Area. By the time Derby had completed its programme of lightweight vehicles, it had produced 122 powered cars and 95 driving trailers. Of these the London Midland Region received 66 motor cars and 55 trailers, while the Eastern and North Eastern Regions had received 56 motor cars and 40 trailers.

Swindon began its output by building twenty-one 3-car sets of Inter-City stock for use between Edinburgh and Glasgow; each set consisted of two powered driving cars with a first-class corridor coach or buffet car in between. They had two AEC 150hp engines in each power car, driving through the standard Wilson four speed gearbox, but unlike the former Derby-built vehicles were of steel construction with a body 64ft 6in long. The motor coaches weighed 38/39 tons each and the trailers 34 tons, making a total of 111 tons for the 3-car set, and providing 158 seats. The coaches were numbered SC79083 to SC79111, SC79155 to SC79168, SC79440 to SC79447 and SC79470 to SC79482, later to be known as Class 126.

The first set was shown to the Minister of Transport at Swindon on the 27 July 1956, but their description

BR Class 116 railcar set with Leyland engines, in use on the Western Region. (*British Rail*)

in the technical press produced a number of protest letters complaining that the feature of being able to see forward by front seat passengers had been abandoned in favour of a full-width driver's compartment. This protest was fairly limited, and it seemed that most passengers were not unduly bothered about this aspect after the first novelty. One strange feature of these sets was that no through air pipe was provided since each car produced its own air supply, but if the leading cars engines were out of commission the horn could not be sounded, which counted as a failure. This was later rectified.

Derby's next venture was to build 50 sets of 2-car units for the Eastern Region. These were steel, 63ft 6in long, but since larger engines were now available they could stick to the one power car arrangement. The Leyland Albion engine rated at 230hp was used in conjunction with the standard transmission, though one car was fitted with a Self Changing Gears automatic transmission and one car had a Rolls Royce 238hp engine with the twin disc torque convertor.

Following the initial schemes in the West Riding and in West Cumberland the latter was soon extended from Carlisle to Whitehaven. The next services were based on Newcastle on Tyne, Manchester and Birmingham for local and suburban types of duty, with Inter-City services between Birmingham and Swansea as well as between Edinburgh and Glasgow.

In 1955 the first diesel training school was opened at Derby with Instructors Mike Adkinson and Dennis Davies. The Eastern Region built new maintenance depots at Lincoln and at Norwich, but still employed the pit system for work on the underfloor equipment, which was not entirely satisfactory. In 1955 also occurred the ASLEF strike which was to lose traffic to the road at a vital time, most of which was never recovered.

By the end of 1956 BR had commissioned some 279 power cars and in June that year Lord Rusholme, the London Midland Region Chairman, had mentioned in

a speech in Liverpool the plans to introduce a fast inter-urban diesel service between Liverpool and Leeds. In anticipation of this, the Carriage & Wagon Department at Derby in conjunction with the Mechanical Engineer had produced two underfloor diesel electric railcars of 450hp each. These used a flat Paxman 6-cylinder 6ZHXL engine (based on the RPH engines previously used in the Fell locomotive, No 10100, and in No 10800 Bo-Bo locomotive) coupled to a BTH main generator and driving one powered bogie to each car. The cars' underframes and bogies were from the former Euston-Watford electric stock built originally in 1926.

The Paxman engine was of 7in (17.8mm) bore by 7.75in (19.7mm) stroke and ran at 1500rpm; it had an aluminium alloy crankcase with aluminium-bronze valve seats, while the crankshaft, camshaft and connecting rods were of steel with copper-lead lined steel shell main and big-end bearings. The total weight of the 2-car set was 103 tons.

Starting in September 1956 these two cars carried out a series of high-speed runs. The first was from Derby to London (St Pancras) 129 miles in 120 minutes, then from Euston to Rugby (82 miles) in 78 minutes. Runs from Derby to Gloucester and back (including the 1 in 37 Lickey Incline climbed at 36mph) were followed by some journeys on the Eastern Region from Sheffield and York to London (Kings Cross) run in even time. These were followed by a regular daily service from Derby to Carlisle, putting up a total of 43,000 miles in seventeen months. In spite of all this effort the equipment was not chosen for any further railcar applications on account of its weight and cost. It was to find its use in the rather unsuccessful Class 17 Bo-Bo 900hp diesel-electric locomotives.

The stock for the Trans-Pennine route, known as Class 124, was not eventually produced until 1960, when it was built by Swindon using the 230hp Albion engine. This engine was also used in the Class 114 units supplied to the Eastern Region, in Class 115 suburban units sent to the London Midland Region, and in Classes 123 (Inter-City pattern) and 128 (Parcel cars), most of which went to the Western Region.

During 1957 Derby produced the first batch of 83 power cars using the Leyland 150hp engine with the

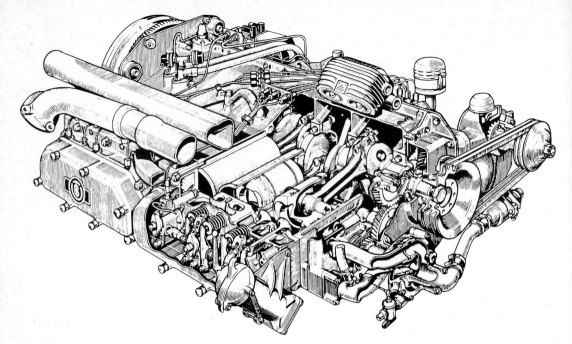

Cut-away view of BUT Leyland engine.

standard Wilson transmission; these all went to the Western Region, based principally on Tyseley and Cardiff for use in the Birmingham area and in the Valleys of South Wales. They were later known as the Class 116 and eventually amounted to 216 power cars, all of which were originally allocated to the Western Region but were recently used on other regions.

The following is a description of the equipment used in the majority of the railcar powered units which included two AEC or Leyland 150hp engines and the Wilson 4-speed gearbox.

The AEC (or A type engine) was a 6-cylinder horizontal model with a bore of 5.12in (142mm) giving 150hp at 1800rpm. The swept volume was 690cu in (11.3 litres) and the weight with its fluid coupling was 1,760lb (800kg). The pistons were deep bowl aluminium alloy with a forged palm ended connecting rod. The fuel injection pump was a block type CAV No NL6F90/60. The fuel system consisted of a tank, filter, lift pump, injection pump and injectors. The water cooling system which was a source of a lot of the troubles associated with this equipment was as shown in Fig 48 and was originally a non-pressurised system with a vent pipe.

An alternative engine used was the Leyland L type R/E 680 with a bore of 5in (127mm) and a stroke of 5.75in (146mm) having a capacity of 677cu in (11.1 litres), also giving 150hp at 1,800rpm. In this case the peak torque was at 1,100rpm against that of 1,400rpm for the AEC engine. The Leyland piston was of the torroidal cavity type, but otherwise the engines were very similar. Each engine is equipped with one exhauster for the vacuum brakes and one compressor for the supply of air for auxiliaries and controls. It was

a great pity that the vacuum brake was retained for these units which would not normally run in conjunction with loco-hauled vacuum braked stock but this type was adopted in case these units were to be used to haul tail traffic such as milk cars or horseboxes. In fact they were hardly ever used for this purpose and even then some operating discipline could have eliminated them. Only on the Southern Region was the Engineering side firm enough to insist on compressed-air braking combined with electric heating on these modern units but then this was to match the equipment to that already used on SR electric units.

For both engines the fluid coupling consisted of two members, the runner connected to the crankshaft and the rear casing connected to the output flange. At idling speed the rear casing is not driven, but begins to take up the drive at around 700rpm.

The Wilson epicyclic 4-speed gearbox consists of three epicyclic gear trains and a multiplate clutch which provides fourth or top gear with a ratio of 1/1. The intermediate gears are obtained by the use of brakes which lock the appropriate annulus, so causing the planet carrier to rotate at a reduced speed. The gear ratios obtained in the various gears were:-

    First gear 4.28/1
    Second gear 2.43/1
    Third gear 1.59/1
    Fourth gear 1.00/1.

In the normal automotive type box a reverse gear is also provided, but this was no use in the railcar since speeds in both directions had to be the same, and a separate reverse device was provided in the final axle drive.

The final drive from the gearbox was by cardan shaft to the driven axle through one of two bevel pinions selected according to the desired direction of

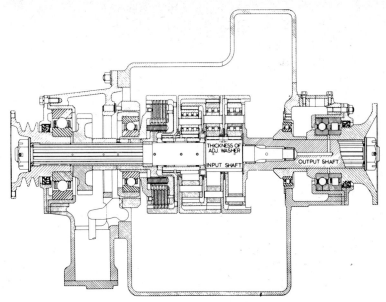

Cross-section of Wilson gearbox.

travel. This selection was achieved by a driving dog moved by a fork which in turn was actuated by an air cylinder. There were a number of weaknesses in this system which were the cause of not a little trouble.

The first weakness was due to the multi-plate clutch in the Wilson gearbox, which tended to rotate the output shaft, particularly with the drag due to cold oil; this made the movement of the dogs difficult since the primary bevel pinion would not come to rest. Secondly, the full air pressure was imposed on the selector piston which caused the striking fork to move with such force as to damage the dog teeth or to fracture the fork itself. This led to a redesign of the fork so as to try to eliminate the weak points. A third problem was that sometimes the air pressure was not enough to ensure

Railcar coupling symbols.

the operation of the selector mechanism and this then had to be carried out from the ground at the coach in question.

There were three cardan shafts used, one from the engine to the gearbox, one from the gearbox to the driving axle and one to the radiator fan drive. The first one embodied a free-wheel device to allow downhill operation at speeds higher than could be obtained with the engine in drive, without causing damage to the engine itself.

The controls consisted of two systems, an electrical method for selection and an air pressure arrangement for actuation.

Because of the variations in the types of transmission not all units could work in multiple and this resulted in five different control systems which were coded so that they could not be joined together in error. These five were:—

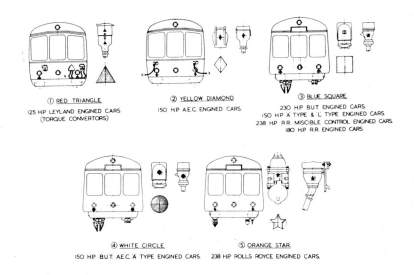

① RED TRIANGLE.
125 H.P. LEYLAND ENGINED CARS.
(TORQUE CONVERTORS)

② YELLOW DIAMOND.
150 H.P. A.E.C. ENGINED CARS.

③ BLUE SQUARE.
230 H.P. B.U.T. ENGINED CARS.
150 H.P. 'A' TYPE & 'L' TYPE ENGINED CARS.
238 H.P. R.R. MISCIBLE CONTROL ENGINED CARS.
180 H.P. R.R. ENGINED CARS.

④ WHITE CIRCLE.
150 H.P. B.U.T. A.E.C 'A' TYPE ENGINED CARS.

⑤ ORANGE STAR.
238 H.P. ROLLS ROYCE ENGINED CARS.

Gear Selection System on Wilson Gearbox
Torque Transmission Diagram

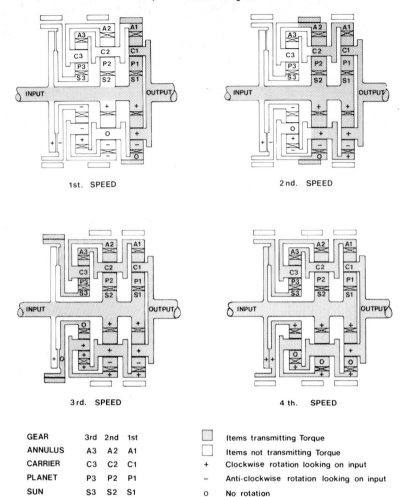

1st. SPEED   2nd. SPEED

3rd. SPEED   4 th. SPEED

GEAR	3rd	2nd	1st			
ANNULUS	A3	A2	A1		Items transmitting Torque	
CARRIER	C3	C2	C1		Items not transmitting Torque	
PLANET	P3	P2	P1	+	Clockwise rotation looking on input	
SUN	S3	S2	S1	−	Anti-clockwise rotation looking on input	
				o	No rotation	

Gear selection system on Wilson gearbox.

Red Triangle. Used for Derby lightweight stock with the Leyland 125hp engine and torque converter. This was also later applied to the Derby-built stock for the Bedford line with Rolls Royce 238hp engines and torque converters.

Yellow Diamond. Used for Derby lightweight and Metro-Cammell stock with AEC 150hp engines with Wilson gearboxes. This was also used for the three Cravens parcel vans with the same power units.

White Circle. Used for the original Swindon Inter-City stock for the Scottish Region with AEC 150hp engines and Wilson gearboxes.

Orange Star. Used for the Derby-built sets with Rolls Royce 238hp engines and torque converter transmission.

Blue Square. Used for all other stock employing the standard transmission with either AEC, Leyland or Rolls Royce engines. They could be of 150hp, 180hp or 230hp according to the power required. This category covered 3,206 out of the 3,810 DMUs provided.

The Blue Square system employed 49 out of the 76 train wires provided by the jumper connections and gave sufficient circuits to provide for the control of six power cars, which would have been sufficient for a 12-coach train. The longest DMU train formation appears to have been a 10-car assembly used for football specials. At first all the EP valves were actuated from the battery in the control car, but the voltage drop down the train was too great to allow reliable operation and this was changed to permit operation from the batteries in individual cars.

The air pressure system actuated the gear selector, the throttle control motors and the direction of motion in the final drive.

By the end of 1956 just over 150 underfloor power cars were in service, mostly of the so called lightweight construction, but from 1957 onward the trend was toward the longer body steel construction weighing

BR Derby lightweight units on a Wembley–Harrow Sunday duty in 1958 (*G. M. Kichenside*)

some six to eight tons more per car. In that same year Swindon started production of its Cross-Country type (Class 120) which amounted to 130 power cars and 64 trailers, of which 21 went to Scotland and the rest to the Western Region. By the end of 1957 the railcar production had amounted to 807 power cars, which were that year joined by the first 20 diesel-electric locomotives from the English Electric and Brush Traction Companies. The railcar fleet included for the first time the initial units of the Southern Region DEMU fleet which are the subject of a separate chapter. Services initiated during 1957 included those from Bradford to Wakefield and from Bolton Abbey to Leeds and Sheffield. In June that year Derby produced its last steam locomotive, No 73154.

1958 opened with Derby completing its 500th railcar in January, and on the 20th of that month the

BR Class 108 4-car set near Oxford. The second coach is a WR Hawksworth corridor composite adapted for dmu use. (*R. H. G. Simpson*)

contract was awarded to J. Laing & Co for the first 53 miles of the M1 motorway from London to Birmingham, at a cost of £15 million. This was probably the biggest nail in the railway coffin since the sale of ex-WD lorries at Slough at the end of World War I, and was to influence the traffic pattern in favour of the heavy road vehicle just when the railways most needed to retain that type of traffic.

During 1958 production started at Derby of 20 power cars using the Rolls Royce 8-cylinder 238hp engine with twin disc transmission (which is described in the next chapter) and which went to the Eastern Region, as well as the first of the Class 108 for which 210 power cars were built, mostly using the Leyland 150hp engine. Of these, the first 43 went to the Eastern Region and the rest to the London Midland. The Eastern Region extended its Bradford services to Goole and to Hull and initiated a new one between Leeds and Pontefract. By the end of 1958 the number of powered railcars was just over 1,400 with only 110 main line diesel-powered locomotives, but the proportion of coaching train miles worked by diesel and electric traction had reached almost 40 percent of the total. This figure had increased to almost 50 percent by the

BR 6-car Trans-Pennine Unit on a Hull–Liverpool working. (*K. Field*)

end of 1959, with a railcar fleet of 1,920 power cars, and during that year Derby started production of the Class 127 high-density stock for the St Pancras to Bedford services. Electrification had been planned for this line way back in the LMS days, combined with a low-level approach to a rebuilt Euston station, but the second World War stopped such ideas and this electrification project was not finally begun until 1977, being completed in 1984. The Class 127 started running to steam timings during 1959 and the full service replacing the steam trains was introduced on 3 January 1960. This involved 60 power cars using the Rolls Royce 238hp engine and 60 trailers, made up in 4-car sets. These 30 sets provided 26 diagrams daily giving a total mileage of 5,205 miles. This would correspond to around 52,000 miles per annum per set, thus giving a total life mileage of 1.2 million miles. As a measure of the problem of providing for a commuter service, the daily diagrams varied between 85 and 450 miles per day.

During 1959 Swindon produced a second batch of 44 power cars for the Scottish Inter-City services (Class 126) and in the next year built the Class 124 for the Trans-Pennine service between Liverpool and Leeds. They consisted of seventeen 3-car units each with one trailer and two power cars fitted with Leyland Albion 230hp engines, made up into 6-car sets. Each 6-car set weighed 228 tons and provided 60 first-class, 232 second-class seats, and a buffet car. The design of the driving car ends was worked out in conjunction with a Design Panel which produced a rounded end, but the window glasses were rather prone to leak or fall out in adverse weather conditions sometimes encountered on those journeys.

During 1960/61 Derby Works produced the last of its railcars in two classes, Class 115 with the 230hp Albion engine as 4-car suburban sets for the LM Region, and Class 107 with AEC 150hp engine as 3-car sets for the Scottish Region. By the time Derby had completed its railcar production this amounted to 832

power cars and 560 trailers, making 1392 in total or just over one third of all railcars produced.

Swindon's last production was in 1963 and included ten sets of 3-car units for Western Region Inter-City services between Cardiff and Portsmouth. These comprised the Class 123 and were the only cars to be fitted with B4 bogies, which gave a vastly superior ride. By the end of its production Swindon had built 272 power cars and 145 trailers, making a total of 417 railcars. The combined production of Derby and Swindon in the ten years from 1953 to 1963 had thus amounted to 1,809 diesel railcars, using 2,208 diesel engines.

By 1963 a combination of electrification and dieselisation had eliminated steam working in the South East of the UK, which included the Eastern Section of the Southern Region and the East Anglian portion of the Eastern Region. This was partly to satisfy the Clean Air stipulations of the City of London and to avoid coal haulage and handling in those areas. It was most unfortunate that just at that moment down came the Beeching Axe with a tremendous swipe regardless of its effect on other related traffic. The logic of the plan was that branch lines cost £77 per week per mile for basic maintenance, that steam trains cost £168 per mile per week and DMUs between £45 and £67, thus a line would not be viable at under 17,000 passengers a week. All routes below this would be closed to save £18 million a year, and in 1964 this resulted in the closure of 134 branch lines including a number in Yorkshire where the first diesel railcar services had been introduced only six to seven years earlier.

In spite of the better service offered by the diesel railcar the growth in the ownership of motor cars in the '*Never had it so good*' years meant that the necessary potential traffic to justify the retention of many branch lines just did not seem to be there. The availability of stock from these closed branches meant a cessation in the building programme since the surplus stock could be switched to other locations to phase out the steam services planned for displacement. Thus out of the 4,600 railcars planned a total of 4,171

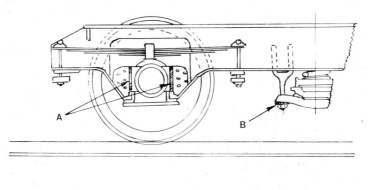

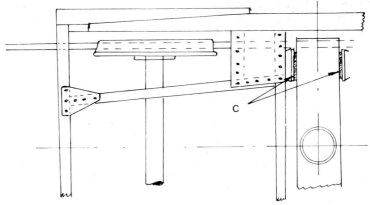

Diagram of railcar bogie, illustrating points of wear leading to poor riding. A – hornguides, B – swing links, C – bolster guide bearings. (*Author*)

was built including the Southern Region DEMUs, the Blue Pullmans and the 4-wheel versions; included in the total was one bogie power car and trailer equipped for battery-electric traction.

The early problems due to inadequate training of staff in the operation and maintenance of these units were by now largely overcome, but a number of other faults showed up in service, one of which was persistent overheating of the engines. The radiators adopted had insufficient margin to cope with the fouling-up due to oil and brake block dust which clogged the cooling matrix and meant frequent steam cleaning or regular replacement at 70,000 miles. This problem was partially overcome by pressurising the system to 5lb/sq in, which enabled the engine temperature to be raised by some 10 degrees; it further reduced coolant losses and obviated topping-up and the costs of anti-freeze addition. Other problems were due to leaks in the air operating control systems and poor electrical insulation; all the original VIR cables had to be replaced by butyl insulated type.

Probably the worst feature of these cars from the operating aspect was the heating method. The electrical system, so successfully adopted by the Southern Region was ruled out because the load on any one engine would have been too great, and provision would have been necessary to counter the loss of any

engine unit. Waste heat recovery was not considered satisfactory after the trials with the LMS 3-car set of 1938, so the only other solution was the use of a separate oil-fired heater. The type adopted was the Smith's warm air heater giving 450cu ft/minute at 50,000BTU/hour. This had a low-voltage glow plug and the fuel was delivered to a spinner which flung the oil into the air stream. The glow plug was a constant source of trouble, becoming heavily coated with carbon from partially burned fuel and so causing earth faults; carbon deposits also formed in the heater passages, thus restricting air flow and making matters even worse. The rich mixture resulted in higher flame temperatures and thus rapid corrosion of the combustion chamber, and though this was partly overcome by the use of stainless steel these heaters usually had to be changed twice during the heating season. Some years later a more powerful Type 2 heater was adopted which gave 600cu ft/min of air at 80,000BTU per hour, and this had the advantage of fuel atomised direct into the air stream as well as a high-voltage spark. This model was superseded by a Type 3 giving 650cu ft of air and had two separate fans for the combustion air and the heating air. Some of the early heater installations suffered from having the air intakes badly sited so that they drew in exhaust from the heater, but they were resited later on.

One other trouble that plagued these units from the outset was due to run-down batteries. The first chargers were DC generators driven from the output of the gearbox or from the trailer bogie axle. They gave inadequate charge at low speed and were ineffective below 18mph. Later they were replaced by CAV alternators, two type AC8 driven from the diesel engines and one type AC14 driven off the trailer axle. They were effective down to 9mph and their output was rectified for the charging function.

During the early years the availability of these units was fairly consistent at around 86 percent, but this fell to 80.3 in 1976 and is still about that figure. Miles per casualty fell from 34,000 to 19,000 in 1966, but are now up to 25,800. The average distance between engine removals for overhaul has been 110,000 miles, with the Rolls Royce showing better at 140,000; of the two BUT 150hp engines the Leyland has been the better, resulting in a replacement programme starting with refurbishing scheme in 1974 whereby the AEC engines were gradually replaced by the Leyland 680H engine rated at 181hp. By 1974 the railway-built DMU power cars were down from the 1,104 to 869, the eliminations coming mainly from the lightweight stock (122) and the Class 126 Inter City stock in Scotland (84) it had been replaced by the double-ended Class 27-hauled MkII vehicles.

The refurbishing scheme started with the Class 102 Metro-Cammell cars, and will be described in the next chapter. Since 1974 the number has come down to 789 power cars with the loss of Class 125 and half of the Trans-Pennine Class 124. Classes 107, 108, 114, 115 and 116 have been refurbished, while the Swindon-built versions have not been included, nor was the St Pancras-Bedford Class 127, due for elimination under the electrification of that line. Most of the trailer cars

from that stock were due for transfer to the West Midland Passenger Transport area.

Due to changes in operating demands many of these railcars have been moved from their original Regions; in particular Class 116 which was exclusively Western has been reallocated to all four Regions, but mainly to the London Midland. Class 120 has also gone from its first homes in Scotland and on the Western Region to the Eastern and Midland Regions, while Class 123 has also migrated to the Eastern Region.

In spite of their faults and weaknesses these railcars have done a good job for British Rail and major complaints from passengers have been about the seats, the riding qualities and the heating system. There have been endless discussions as to whether to provide high or low backed seats and this is to some extent determined by the type of duty for which these vehicles are used. Generally speaking the above floor design and layout was of three patterns – General Purpose, Inter-City, and Suburban. Multiple units for suburban work had side doors to each seating bay, with three-plus-two seating astride the off centre passageway. Gangway connections were not originally provided but many sets have had them fitted in recent years to allow access through the train to the toilets in the trailer car and for conductor guard operation. The general purpose units were gangwayed within the set, had three-plus-two seats in the second class, but had only two passenger doors on each side. Units for long distance services were more akin to locomotive hauled coaches with two-plus-two seating and some types were gangwayed right through the unit.

4 Industrial-Built DMU stock

Considering the bogie DMU railcars as a whole, those built by the private industrial firms were slightly in excess of those built by the British Rail Workshops at Derby and Swindon. The total number built by the private builders was 2,001 against 1,809 built by BR and these were all built between 1956 and 1960.

The first private venture into the DMU field was by the British United Traction Company in 1952 when it produced some 4-wheel lightweight cars powered by an AEC 125hp diesel engine with the Wilson 4-speed gearbox. These were demonstrated on the Gerrards Cross line and later went into service near Wellingborough. They spent most of their life on the Watford-St Albans line and were withdrawn in 1963. These strictly come in the category of the railbus and

Table 1 – comparison of railcar structures

will be considered in more detail in that section.

In 1954 it was realised that the total requirements of diesel railcars would be beyond the capacity of the British Rail Workshops, so a review was undertaken of the construction capabilities of the private carriage builders in the UK who were asked to submit designs and tenders for a limited range of body and seating layouts in two categories, namely 57ft 0in and 63ft 6in according to the various Regional needs. Since by that date the BUT 150hp and the Rolls-Royce 180hp engines had become available, construction was confined to all-steel bodies to avoid the extra expense involved in the use of aluminium alloys. The general specification included the following provisions:

(a) Vehicles to be 57ft 0in long and to conform to C1 loading gauge.
(b) To withstand not less than 80 tons end load and an

Table I.—Comparison of vehicle structures of various 57ft motor second brake diesel railcars

Builder	Type of Construction		Vehicle Tare Weight Tons
	Body	*Underframe*	
Cravens	Pressed steel framing members of welded construction, with 16 SWG panelling. Certain body and underframe members of 'Corten' steel.	Fabricated from folded steel plate section, comprising double solebar with channel and box section crossbar and bolster. Portion of framing adapted to form fuel tanks.	30·0
Metropolitan Cammell Carriage & Wagon	Pillars of $\frac{1}{8}$in thick pressed steel channel section, with 16 SWG bodyside panelling. Roof framing and panelling of light alloy.	Combination of rolled steel sections and pressings, the main members being riveted together. Solebar a deep pressing incorporating the body-side curb rail. Longitudes are 8in deep pressings.	32·0
Park Royal Vehicles	Framing a combination of light alloy and steel members, with 16 SWG light alloy panelling.	Channel section solebars, longitudes and crossbars in mild steel, with riveted joints.	33·5
Birmingham Railway Carriage & Wagon	Fully integral body/underframe structure, comprising mild steel channel section solebars and longitudes surmounted by pressed steel framing members, all of welded construction. Panelling of 16 SWG steel.		31·0
Gloucester Railway Carriage & Wagon	Fully integral body/underframe structure. Below floor level, main members generally of tubular construction. Solebars built up of upper and lower mild steel tubes, $\frac{1}{8}$in thick, with inner and outer web plates. Cross bars of rectangular tubes in 10 SWG sheet steel. No inner longitudinal members between bolsters. Above floor level, pillars of 2in × 2in 'Fortiweld' tube, tapering in thickness from 12 SWG at bottom to 14 SWG at top. Doorway pillars of special tubular section with extruded alloy check strip. Panelling of 14 SWG 'Corten' steel.		30·3
D. Wickham	Fully integral body/underframe structure. All framing members of $2\frac{3}{8}$in × $2\frac{3}{8}$in × 10 SWG mild steel square tubing. Panelling of 16 SWG light alloy.		27·0
British Railways, Derby (Light alloy)	Fully integral body/underframe structure almost entirely of light alloy extruded sections, cold formed riveted. Bodyside panelling of 10 SWG light alloy, riveted to frame members.		27·0

Metro-Cammell 2-car diesel unit in PTE livery approaching York. (*G. M. Kichenside*)

evenly distributed vertical load three times the normal load.

(c) Bogies to be of 8ft 6in wheelbase with 3ft 0in diameter wheels and roller-bearing axleboxes.

(d) Open type body with good all-round visibility.

(e) Power/weight ratio of 10/1 for motor cars and 6/1 for motor car plus trailer.

(f) Transmission to be suitable for 65mph maximum and for six hours' continuous operation.

(g) Underfloor fuel capacity for 500 miles.

(h) Automatic oil-fired heating.

(i) Capacity to multiple up to eight vehicles with deadman protection.

Seven firms contributed towards this programme and these were in order of quantities:

Metropolitan-Cammell Carriage & Wagon Company	760
Birmingham Railway Carriage & Wagon Company	437
Cravens Limited	405
Gloucester Railway Carriage & Wagon Company	200
Pressed Steel Company	149
Park Royal Vehicles	40
D. Wickham & Company	10
	2001

Taking them in order of production, the first vehicles into service were lightweight cars built by Metro-Cammell in 1956 consisting of 36 power cars and 36 trailers; they were not strictly part of the major programme since they weighed only 26.5 tons for the motor brake seconds and 25 tons for the driving trailers. The motor coaches had the two AEC 150hp engines with the standard Wilson 4-speed gearbox to each power car. Of these, 29 sets of two cars went to the Eastern Region to inaugurate services in East Anglia and the other seven to the London Midland Region for the Bury to Bacup line in Lancashire.

Metropolitan-Cammell Carriage & Wagon Co

Table 1 shows the various makes and types of vehicles

supplied to the standard specification, and out of these the most numerous type was what became Class 101 produced by Metro-Cammell, totalling 439 cars of which 258 were powered. These cars used the AEC 150hp engine with standard transmission and were distributed among the North Eastern, London Midland and Scottish Regions. Similar vehicles fitted with the Leyland 150hp engine were originally known as Class 102, but these are now all included in Class 101, though most have now had Leyland engines fitted. The total of the two classes came to 637 vehicles distributed as 356 to the North Eastern, 122 to the Midland and 159 to Scotland. They are generally regarded as the most successful of all the railcars produced and will probably outlast most of the others. They weighed 32 tons for the motors cars and 25 tons for the trailer cars.

Metro-Cammell also produced 51 cars of Class 111 using the Rolls-Royce 180hp engine in conjunction with a 4-speed transmission manufactured by the Self Changing Gear Company, and in this case the motor cars weighed one ton more at 33 tons. Most went to the North Eastern Region.

The manufacturer's description of the cars built to these Classes 101, 102 and 111 is that the body structure was of the integral type, all units being jig-built to ensure interchangeability. The side framing extends as a complete unit from below the underframe into the roof portion, with the steel side panels spot-welded to the structure and sprayed internally with asbestos as a precaution against condensation and noise. The roof frames and panels were of aluminium, but the body ends were of steel with openings for gangways, or in the case of the driving ends, having three windows.

The steel underframes were made up of rolled sections with fabricated end frames including headstock and bolsters. The buffers on the first units had rubber springs, but the rest were fitted with the oleo-pneumatic type. The passenger and driver's doors were interchangeable with those on the then current main line steam-hauled stock.

Seating was arranged with two seats on each side of the central gangway in the first class, while in the second class most seats were two on one side and three on the other; seats were finished in blue in the first-class and in green or maroon in the second. A typical 2-car unit provided 12 first and 104 second class seats. Heating was by the usual Smith's oil-burning air heater, with ducting along the floor to apertures below the seats. A lavatory was provided at the gangway end of the driving trailer car.

Since the Rolls-Royce engines were first used in the Class 111 cars a description of those engines with their associated transmission and control systems is included at this point. The Rolls-Royce C series diesel engines were built in 6- or 8-cylinder formation as in-line engines, and they could be supercharged or turbocharged; they could also be supplied in vertical or horizontal form. The C engine range was of 5.125in (130.2mm) bore by 6in (152.4mm) stroke and ran at 1800rpm, with a piston speed of 1,800ft per minute. The crank case was of cast-iron with a chrome-molybdenum nitrided crankshaft and with connecting rods of the same material. The pistons were of aluminium alloy with a combustion cavity and four rings, three compression and one oil scraper. The main and big-end bearings were thin-wall lead bronze with lead-indium facings. The cast-iron cylinder heads, cast in groups of three or four, were fitted with stellite-face valve inserts with phosphor-bronze guides and copper injector sleeves. The lubrication system was of the wet

Interior of refurnished Metro-Cammell Class 102 unit. (*BR*)

sump type with full-flow AC filters; the sump capacity was 7.5 gallons for the 6-cylinder engine and 12.5 gallons for the 8-cylinder version.

The 6-cylinder naturally-aspirated model (C6N FLH) gave 180hp at a BMEP rating of 109lb/sq in and this could also give 233hp when supercharged, or 262hp in turbocharged form. The model fitted in the Class 111 stock was the C6N FLH which had a weight of 2,814lb (1,276kg) including the fluid coupling, and was in the horizontal version with the cylinders at an inclination of 17.5 degrees to the horizontal. In this version the standard 4-speed epicyclic transmission system was used in conjunction with the BUT control system and these could multiple with other similarly controlled stock having the blue square code.

Similar power units were also fitted in the Class 110 cars supplied by the Birmingham Railway Carriage & Wagon Company, but the other Rolls-Royce engines of the 8-cylinder type (C8N FLH) rated at 238hp were fitted in the Class 127 sets built at Derby and in the single-engine cars built by Craven Ltd.

This 8-cylinder version, which weighed 4,800lb (2,178kg) including the torque convertor, was used in conjunction with a Lysholm-Smith torque convertor built by Rolls-Royce under licence from the Twin Disc Clutch Company of the USA. It seems ironic that a British company should have to build under licence a system that was originally developed in the UK, but today, that seems typical of British business. The torque convertor was the model DFR 10000 Ms500 hydrokinetic 3-stage with a torque potential of 500lb/ft. The operating clutches were multi-plate oil-cooled and actuated by oil pressure from the lubricating oil pump which gave up to 150lb/sq in working pressure. The converter fluid was the diesel

fuel from the main fuel tanks which could reach a pressure of 65lb/sq in and had a normal operating temperature of 220deg F with a limit of 250deg for three minutes. Since this was well above the flash point for this type of fuel, it was a source of potential fire risk which unfortunately happened too often. This operating fluid has now been changed to the same as that used in the lubricating system.

The shaft drive and final axle drive were similar to those on the other railcars, but because the torque converter was more compact than the 4-speed transmission arrangement only one shaft was required, and this was considerably longer than those used with the standard system. This was also to cause problems later due to the bending of these shafts, which were later modified by the fitting of a silicon-manganese torsion bar and a viscous damper.

The four versions of cars built by Metro-Cammell, its lightweight and Classes 101, 102 and 111 amounted to 760 vehicles, and they were distributed as 58 to the Eastern Region (lightweight) 407 to the North Eastern, 136 to the London Midland and 159 to the Scottish Region, all produced between 1957 and 1960 an average of almost four cars per week. After the initial lightweight sets the next batches went to the West Riding of Yorkshire and to the Darlington area. The first of the Class 111 with the Rolls-Royce engines went to Manchester, with later ones to the Leeds area; these seem to be recognised as the best of the DMU engines with mileages up to 240,000 between replacements.

Some other data pertaining to the Metro-Cammell Classes 101/2 are:—

Tractive Effort		
First gear	6,570lb	Max speed 15.3mph
Second gear	3,710lb	Max speed 27.0mph
Third Gear	2,420lb	Max speed 41.0mph
Top Gear	1,610lb	Max speed 65.5mph

Wheelbase	48ft 6in
Bogie wheelbase	8ft 6in
Wheel diameter	3ft 0in
Fuel capacity	80 gallons for engines
	25 gallons for heaters
Fuel injectors	CAV BDL L150
Compressor	Clayton Type PCGA189
Exhauster	Clayton Type C725

The drivers' instructions relating to gear changing were as follows:—

Changing-up
When the engine speed indicator shows CHANGE UP
1. Return throttle to IDLING
2. Allow engine speed indicator needle to fall to between CHANGE UP and CHANGE DOWN.
3. Select next higher gear.
4. PAUSE FOR TWO SECONDS then re-open throttle.
5. Change gear progressively in this manner until TOP gear is reached.

Changing-down
When the engine speed indicator shows CHANGE DOWN
1. Return throttle to IDLING
2. Select LOWER gear
3. PAUSE FOR TWO SECONDS and re-open throttle.

One of the complaints by the Western Region concerns the driving techniques when its DMUs on the Reading to Gatwick service are handled by Southern Region drivers, who are reputed to drive them as though they were diesel-electrics instead of adopting the procedure outlined above.

In 1974, after nearly 20 years of service, the time

Cravens-built 2-car Class 105 unit in Ribblesdale. (*BR*)

came for a refurbishing programme and the first set selected for this treatment was a Metro-Cammell class 102 unit, Car Nos 51451, 59545 and 51518. It was repainted white with yellow ends and a broad blue band along the sides of the coaches below the windows. Power car No 51518 was given the 'medium cost' treatment (£6,000) which included nine first-class Inter-City type seats in place of the previous twelve, wall-to-wall carpets and a double row of fluorescent lighting. The second-class seats were modified to carry individual cushions. New heating thermostats set to 70deg F were installed, with improved air intake position to avoid drawing-in exhaust fumes to the heater intake. The engine mountings have also been improved using a rubber/metal sandwich in shear and better silencers were installed. The other two cars were give the 'low cost' treatment (£1,000 per car) which included seat re-covering, new linoleum flooring, new gangway curtains and fluorescent lighting as well as the improvements to the engine mounting and silencing.

This 3-car set was for demonstration to the various newly-formed Passenger Transport Authorities, which would be expected to contribute towards the refurbishing costs for units in their areas. Demonstrations were given at Marylebone, Birmingham, Derby, Chester, Liverpool, Manchester, Preston, Carlise and Southampton, with the idea of renovating some 1,800 of the DMU fleet.

Eventually the choice was for the 'low cost' refurbishing scheme, and to date most of the Metro-Cammell cars in Classes 101, 102 and 111 have been completed. After the first initial painting scheme with the blue band had been dubbed the 'Stork treatment' the finish was changed to the standard two-tone blue/grey of the Inter-City trains, though not all cars have so far been finished to this standard. This can

result in a mix of three different systems of painting which can create odd-looking train sets.

The Metro-Cammell Class 101, which now includes both 101 and 102 classes, is by far the most numerous currently in use comprising 352 power cars out of the 364 first built; most of these are in the Eastern Region (150), but they are distributed among all Regions except the Southern and are appreciated as reliable performers.

Birmingham Railway Carriage & Wagon Company

The second largest private producer of the DMU railcars was BRCW of Smethwick in Staffordshire, which turned out a total of 437 vehicles in Classes 104, 110 and 118, of which 269 were power cars. The allocation of these cars was 174 to the North Eastern Region, 218 to the London Midland, and 45 to the Western. Classes 104 and 110 were 57ft 6in long. Class 104 used Leyland engines while Class 110 was fitted with Rolls-Royce 180hp engines. Class 118 had suburban type 64ft 0in bodies and also used the Leyland 150hp engines.

BRCW commenced production in 1957 and finished the last of Class 110 in 1961; the later versions of this class were equipped with 4-character headcode panels. They pioneered the use of fibreglass mouldings for the roof ends of the driving compartment, and also used fibreglass for the header tanks in the engine cooling system, where it was the cause of quite a few problems. BRCW also made extensive use of fibreglass in the Classes 25, 27 and 33, diesel-electric locomotives that it built. The company had just completed prototype 2,750hp diesel-electric locomotive D0260 *Lion* when it went into liquidation largely as a consequence of taking on a considerable order for London Transport rolling stock at an unremunerative price.

The BRCW product range as a whole was of good quality and most of its original railcars are still in service. In 1974 only nine out of 269 power cars had

Class 100 unit in dark green/white 'preserved' livery, on the North Yorkshire Moors Railway. (*R. H. G. Simpson*)

GRCW Class 122 single car No M55004 at Stourbridge Town in 1983. The livery is BR blue. Note the prominent exhaust pipes rising to roof level. (*R. N. Pritchard*)

been withdrawn and at the time of this book there were 213 power cars still at work. Class 118 was the only one with no withdrawals, all 30 of the original power cars (Nos W51302–W51331) still being in service on the Western Region.

Cravens Railway Carriage & Wagon Company Sheffield

Later known as just Cravens Ltd, it had produced in 1956 two special first-class and second-class saloon carriages for British Railways embodying many novel features such as reclinable seats, folding tables, double-glazed windows with intermediate venetian blinds, fluorescent lighting and pressure ventilation. The design was not multiplied although a number of detailed features seen on coaches of later years may have been inspired by the prototypes, but Cravens did receive orders for 405 railcars of which 278 were powered and 127 were trailer cars. The power cars included 100 single-engine vehicles, each fitted with one Rolls-Royce 238hp engine. Of these 50 were fitted with the standard mechanical transmission and 50 with the twin disc torque converters. These vehicles, all of which have been withdrawn, carried numbers M51681 to M51780. Cravens also produced three parcels vans Nos M55997–9, which have also been withdrawn.

The other Cravens railcars were all of the 57ft 6in type and became Classes 105 and 106. Class 105 cars were originally fitted with AEC 150hp engines and Class 106 with Leyland engines, but they are all now

Class 105. The original allocations were 50 power cars and 50 trailers to the Eastern Region, 32 to the North Eastern with 31 trailers, 71 to the Midland with 24 trailers, and 22 of each type to Scotland. This stock was not the most popular in the Regions to which it was allocated and has been described as 'rattling itself to bits'. The experiences with the single-engine stock was even worse, with one being involved in a serious fire while on the Bedford to St Pancras service. These units had been used on this suburban service in order to run over the Widened Lines to Moorgate, for which the 64ft 0in Class 127 stock was deemed to be too long. On 12 June one of these cars fitted with mechanical transmission seized its gearbox between Harpenden and St Albans, causing the gearbox casing to break loose from its mouldings; the cardan shaft then ruptured the fuel tank which was located around the shaft and the hot metal ignited the fuel. In the confusion due to a locked gangway door some passengers jumped from the train, two being killed.

It was later found possible to run Class 127 stock over the Widened Lines and the Cravens units were then removed from the Bedford services and used between Kentish Town and Barking. These units were the ones fitted with the torque converter transmission, and since the operating speeds on that line rarely reached 46mph (which was the speed at which direct drive was initiated) they were running almost entirely in converter drive. This resulted in considerable overheating of the converter fluid which was fed back to the main tank on expansion and caused overheating in the main fuel tank. Several fires resulted in these vehicles, and with the other unsatisfactory features caused them to be withdrawn by 1970. They never received an official classification and were not wept over when lost to traffic.

The Class 106 which went to the Eastern Region

GRCW-built Class 128 parcels van. Note corridor connection and split route indicator panels each side. (*R. H. G. Simpson*)

originally had been intended for the former Midland & Great Northern line, which would have involved some fairly long cross-country runs, but the closure of that line in 1959 caused them to be transferred to the Kings Cross suburban service. They proved most unsuitable for those duties; being 2-car units they were underpowered for frequent stopping and starting and thus tended to overheat. Worse still, they were introduced in the hot summer of 1959 and extra water cans had to be available at each station for topping-up en route. Overheating also resulted in low oil pressure, and the safety cut-out relays had themselves to be cut out to keep the service in operation. All were eliminated by 1974, and of the Class 105 only 76 power cars were in service in the early 1980s with a forecast of early withdrawal since they are not included in the refurbishing scheme. Eleven Cravens-built cars are in use as departmental units. M55997 (ex-Class 129 parcels van) is in use for transmission research. Six driving trailers from Class 105 are used as Sandite spray vehicles and two 2-car sets from Class 105 are used for general duties.

Gloucester Railway Carriage & Wagon Company

This firm produced exactly 200 railcars in four categories. The cars which were to become Class 100 were 57ft 6in long had AEC 150hp engines and standard transmission; the class comprised 40 power cars and 40 trailers. The others were 64ft 6in long and included 81 in Class 119 and 29 in Class 122, all with AEC engines. Finally, there were ten parcels vans in Class 128 which were fitted with Albion 230hp engines. The original distribution was 26 to the London Midland, 58 to the Scottish and 116 to the Western Regions. All were produced between 1957 and 1959.

These cars were all of the low-density category and provided cross-country services in Scotland, in Wales and in the Border Country. Since these types of service are prone to cuts and changes of policy they have had many changes in routes and locations. By 1974 the numbers of powered cars had been reduced to 25 for Class 100, 52 for Class 119, 15 for Class 122, while one of the Class 128 had been allotted Class 131 and transferred to Scotland.

The current numbers in service are as follows:–

Class 100   17 on the London Midland Region
Class 119   77 on the Western Region
Class 122   10 on the Midland and Scottish Regions
Class 128   5 on the Midland and Western Regions
Class 131   1 on the Scottish Region

In addition, there is a pair of 2-car sets ex-Class 100 in use on Derby Departmental stock for inspection vehicles as well as five of the Class 122 power cars on Departmental stock as route learners. Class 122 is one of the two classes with driver's controls at each end so that they can be run as single units for light branch lines.

Pressed Steel Company

This firm, which was a subsidiary of the British Motor Corporation, produced Roadrailer vehicles for freight services at its Linwood factory in Scotland as well as passenger vehicles for the Glasgow electrified lines. Its output of 149 diesel railcars was allocated to the Western Region. All were 64ft 0in vehicles in Classes 117 and 121.

Class 117 is high-density stock in 3-car units with two power cars per set. Sets have seats for 230 passengers, weigh 102 tons, and are used for suburban traffic. Class 121 were built for single-unit country duties, but could have a driving trailer added to make 2-car units for the same work. Out of the 84 power cars built for Class 117 82 are still in service. All were fitted with Leyland engines from the outset, but this class is not due for the refurbishing treatment. In Class 121 there are still 15 out of the original 16 power cars and

Pressed Steel Co 3-car unit, Class 117, near Bromsgrove in 1983. The unit is in BR blue-and-grey livery with full yellow ends, and route indicator panels blanked-out. (*R. N. Pritchard*)

Park Royal unit, Class 103, leaving Barmouth. Note all-blue livery, full yellow end, destination indicator and 2-digit route indicator panel. (*R. H. G. Simpson*)

Table 2

Railcar classification and numbers

Builder	Class	Motor cars	Trailer cars	Built	1983	ER	LMR	ScR	WR
Derby	LW	122	95	217					
Derby	107	52	26	78	77		1	76	
Derby	108	210	123	333	306	71	235		
Derby	114	50	50	100	90	90			
Derby	115	82	82	164	160		160		
Derby	116	216	104	320	299	12	186	30	71
Derby	125	40	20	60					
Derby	127	60	60	120	106		106		
A. Derby total		832	560	1,392	1,038	173	688	106	71
Swindon	120	130	64	194	180	96	84		
Swindon	123	20	20	40	33	33			
Swindon	124	34	17	51	35	35			
Swindon	126	88	44	132	6			6	
B. Swindon total		272	145	417	254	164	84	6	
C. BR total (A + B)		1,104	705	1,809	1,292	337	772	112	71
GRCW	100	40	40	80	17		17		
GRCW	119	56	25	81	77				77
GRCW	122	20	9	29	10		5	5	
GRCW	128	10		10	6		3	1	2
Met Cam	LW	36	36	72					
Met Cam	101	364	273	637	611	276	130	161	44
Met Cam	111	47	4	51	44	44			
BRCW	104	179	123	302	175	8	166	1	
BRCW	110	60	30	90	83	83			
BRCW	118	30	15	45	45				45
Cravens	105	175	127	302	140	112	17	11	
Cravens	PV	3		3					
Cravens	U/C	100		100					
PSC	117	84	39	123	121				121
PSC	121	16	10	26	23				23
Park Royal	103	20	20	40	5		5		
Wickham	U/C	5	5	10					
D. Industry total		1,245	756	2,001	1,357	523	343	179	312
Overall total (C + D)		2,349	1,461	3,810	2,649	860	1,115	291	383

they have had their AEC engines replaced by Leyland units; nearly all have been refurbished. The remaining power car from Class 121 (W55035) is in use as a route-learning car in departmental stock under number TDB975659.

Park Royal Vehicles

Park Royal had started by building bus bodies for the London General Omnibus Company and in 1933 had launched into the railway business by building the

RAILCARS COMPARATIVE TABLE BASED ON 6-CAR FORMATIONS

Railcars Comparative Table based on 6-car formations

Class		Builder	Type*	Body Length (ft)	Weight Tons	Seats	Engine hp	HP/ ton	HP/ seat
100	GRCW		LD	57.5	165	324	900	5.4	2.4
101	Met Cam		LD	57.5	171	350	900	5.3	2.6
102	Met Cam		LD	57.5	178	390	1,200	6.7	3.1
103	Pk Royal		LD	57.5	180	348	900	5.0	2.6
104	BRCW		LD	57.5	165	324	900	5.4	2.8
105	Craven		LD	57.5	160	345	900	5.3	2.6
107	Derby		LD	58.0	195	376	1,200	6.2	3.2
108	Derby		LD	57.5	153	360	900	5.9	2.5
110	BRCW		LD	57.5	177	408	1,440	8.1	3.5
111	Met Cam		LD	57.0	174	327	1,440	8.3	4.4
114	Derby		HD	64.5	194	408	1,380	7.1	3.4
115	Derby		HD	64.5	204	444	1,380	6.8	3.1
116	Derby		HD	64.5	197	464	1,200	6.1	2.6
117	PS Co		HD	64.0	204	460	1,200	6.0	2.6
118	BRCW		HD	64.0	204	460	1,200	6.0	2.6
119	GRCW		LD	64.5	210	336	1,200	5.7	3.6
120	Swindon		CC	64.5	206	256	1,200	5.8	4.7
121	P S Co		LD	64.5	224	390	1,800	8.0	4.6
122	GRCW		LD	64.5	210	390	1,800	8.6	4.6
123	Swindon		IC	65.0	212	324	1,200	5.7	3.7
124	Swindon		IC	64.5	228	300	1,840	8.1	6.1
125	Derby		HD	64.5	216	480	1,904	8.8	4.0
126	Swindon		IC	64.5	222	316	1,200	5.4	3.8
127	Derby		HD	64.0	207	546	1,428	6.9	2.6
128	GRCW		PV	64.5	246	—	1,380	5.6	—
201	Eastleigh		LD	58.0	225	252	1,000	4.4	4.0
202	Eastleigh		LD	64.5	231	288	1,000	4.3	3.5
203	Eastleigh		LD	64.5	236	249	1,000	4.2	4.0
205	Eastleigh		LD	64.0	242	219	1,200	4.9	5.5
206	Eastleigh		LD	58/64	238	280	1,200	5.0	4.3
207	Eastleigh		HD	64.0	238	368	1,200	5.0	3.3
Blue Pullman			IC	66.0	299	132	2,000	6.7	15.1
HST (7-car)			IC	75.5	385	369	4,500	11.7	12.7
APT-U (1 + 6)			IC	68.9	265	335	3,000	11.3	8.9

```
*  LD = low-density.
   HD = high-density.
   IC = Inter-City.
   PV = Parcels van.
```

body for the first of the AEC railcars for the Great Western Railway. The firm next came on the railcar scene by building some bodies for eleven 4-wheeled vehicles supplied to the London Midland Region in 1952, which were followed by five railbuses for the Scottish Region in 1958.

In 1957 Park Royal built 40 bogie railcars for the London Midland Region, 20 of which were powered cars fitted with AEC 150hp engines and the standard 4-speed Wilson gearbox. They proved to have body

Two 2-car general purpose dmus built by D. Wickham & Co, seen here at Kings Lynn. Only five units of this type were built for BR; they were later sold or converted as departmental inspection units or withdrawn. (*G. M. Kichenside*)

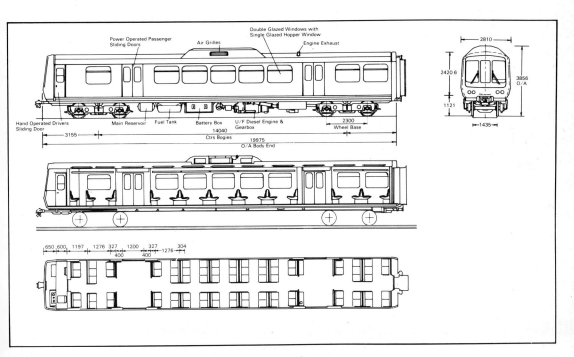

Diagram of the prototype Metro-Cammell Class 151 unit. (*Metro-Cammell Ltd*)

weaknesses and by 1972 only 12 of the power cars were still in service. Two had gone to Derby for use as viaduct inspection vehicles, one of which is now employed for instrumentation tests.

A 2-car set was involved in floods in North Wales in 1976 and was marooned at Llanrwst for a week. In the same year two of the 2-car sets went to the West Somerset Railway. There are still two sets of these Class 103 units in service on the LM Region, but due for withdrawal.

D. Wickham & Company of Ware

D. Wickham & Co, whose premises are in the country area of Hertfordshire, specialises in the production of small rail vehicles of various sorts for all parts of the world. The firm built five railbuses for the Scottish Region in 1958, but before that it produced five 2-car lightweight sets for the Eastern Region.

The power cars were fitted with Leyland 150hp engines with the standard mechanical transmission and control gear. The bodywork was unusual in that no underframe was used, and the all-steel skeleton formed a tubular stress-bearing girder designed to take the various loadings imposed. The framework was built-up from hollow square steel tubing closed to the atmosphere so that no internal corrosion could occur. This body design was evolved for special lightweight cars for South America and resulted in a body frame weighing only 5.3 tons. The trailer car was shown in skeleton form by British Railways at its exhibition of rolling stock at Battersea.

The complete 2-car units weighed 47.2 tons and carried 125 passengers. They were used for branch line duties in East Anglia, but two of the sets were soon withdrawn and sold to Trinidad where lightweight construction was a requirement for export orders. The other sets remained in service until 1970 when they were withdrawn owing to the high cost of maintaining this type of body when it was involved in minor accidents.

DMU Summary

That completes the DMU story as far as the supply of the orginal equipment is concerned; the current situation in April 1984 is shown in Table 2 on page 45 which indicates that of the 3,810 railcars supplied some 2,649 are in use, or just under 70 percent. This is a little better than for the diesel main line locomotives where the corresponding figure is 65 percent. The present average annual mileage per unit is quoted as 55,000 with some sets doing up to 90,000 miles. The figures for miles per casualty vary from 10,000 for the Scottish and Western Regions to 16,000 for the Eastern and 20,000 for the Midland Regions. Engine replacements are now by failure rather than by regular mileage figures as this is reckoned to be more economical.

It is considered that all these units will soon have to be replaced on account of bodywork and the desire to eliminate all stock in which blue asbestos was used for insulation – this is scheduled to take place by 1987.

New designs of DMU are in preparation – both in four-wheel form (see Chapter 9) and bogie types. It is hoped that with better bogies now available and with the lessons learnt concerning engine mountings, controls and cooling systems as well as the coach heating methods, that a comfortable and reliable generation of railcars will be produced. Current prototypes under construction include Class 150 being built at Derby and Class 151 being built by Metro-Cammell; both are designed to use the Leyland engine with the new RRE5 reversing gearbox and varying transmissions; it is hoped that prototypes will be on rail by the time this book appears in print.

5 Diesel-electric multiple-units

Some DEMUs (diesel electric multiple units) were included in the original 1951 Bowles Report for the Hampshire Areas of the Southern Region, but because of demands for a better service on the Hastings line the first units were introduced on that line before the Hampshire units went into service.

In 1955 thirty-two coaches were under construction for the Hastings line intended for steam haulage, and were being built to the special restrictions imposed on this line by the tunnels between Tunbridge Wells and Hastings, particularly those at Grove, Strawberry Hill and Mountfield. Because of poor initial construction these tunnels had to have an extra inner layer of brickwork added at a later date thus restricting the nominal 6ft 0in distance between the running rails to 4ft 8in and so limiting the coach body width to 8ft 0¼in. This did not matter in the years before the Grouping since the standard SECR coach body width was 8ft, but since then the advent of 9ft wide coaches generally has required special narrow bodied stock for this line.

By 1955 increasing loads were making timekeeping almost impossible with steam operation owing to the many speed restrictions imposed by the sharp curves and steep grades on this former South Eastern & Chatham line which had suffered from a shortage of cash during its construction. The ideal solution would have been electrification of the line from Tonbridge to St Leonards (to which the electrified line had already arrived via the coast route in the 1930s) but this still would need special stock for that portion of track. The priority in the 1950s was to complete the planned Phase 2 of the electrification scheme to Dover and the rest of the South Eastern Division of the Southern Region and this meant that the line to Hastings could not be electrified until 1963 at the earliest. Urgent action was needed, and a decision was arrived at on 1 April 1955 to construct seven 6-car diesel-electric units to work the business services from the summer of 1957.

The design of these units was based on some 5-car diesel-electric sets that had been supplied to the Egyptian State Railways in 1947, using the 4-cylinder version of the 10in bore English Electric diesel engine as fitted in the LMS 1,600hp main line locomotive No 10000, The Egyptian contract, which was the first for the new English Electric engine range, included 49 of the 4-cylinder version known as the 4SRKT and 13 of the 16-cylinder model then originally designated 16SVT. Since the takeover of English Electric by GEC this engine range is now known as the Ruston RKC3T,

the latest version of which in 12-cylinder form producing 3,500hp or 292hp per cylinder, is now being fitted in the BR Class 58 freight locomotive.

In 1955 this 4-cylinder engine was designed to produce 500hp at 850rpm, the same output per cylinder as the 16-cylinder power unit fitted in the last of the Southern Region's main line diesels, the 2000hp No 10203, completed in 1954. Calculation showed that with two power cars giving 1,000hp for a 6-car set the journey time between London and Hastings could be reduced by 11 minutes thus giving the long desired 90-minute schedule with four stops for the 62½ miles. For most of the day the timetable worked out at 95 minutes, including nine stops. In order to check that these sets would not be underpowered it was calculated that even a 50 percent increase in power would reduce the difficult 29 minutes between Crowhurst and Tunbridge Wells by only 1½ minutes. The designed performance gave a top speed of 69mph on level track and 40mph on a grade of 1 in 100 (1%).

The English Electric 4-cylinder 4SRKT engine was a cast-iron structure with a 4-valve cylinder head and a low-level camshaft which operated the valves through push rods, as well as the individual fuel pumps. The pistons were cast in aluminium alloy with five rings and a combustion crown that became known as the Mexican Hat pattern. The connecting rods were forged but not machined, and were of the inclined bolt design; ten of the first engines were supplied with the earlier pattern of parallel bolt rod, but they were soon changed for the later type. A Lanchester balancer gear was fitted to reduce vibration, since the power car was arranged to accommodate passengers. The governor was the English Electric type arranged for electric step-speed control with a special low-speed running step for when the electric heating was in use. The main generator was the English Electric EE 824/26 and the traction motors were the standard Southern Region type EE507 rated at 250hp for one hour with a gear ratio of 65/16. The two traction motors per power car were installed in the rear bogie of that car to keep the axle load down on the leading bogie. An auxiliary generator rated at 13.2kW supplies the control and lighting circuits at 90volts, and this is capable of working in parallel with the 110volt equipment now standard on other diesel and electric stock. The heating load is supplied from the main generator at up to 800volts and the load of 50kW for each three coaches is supplied from the power unit at that end of the train. Since the heat supplied at the idling speed of 450rpm

400hp diesel-electric railcar unit, with English Electric 4-cylinder engine, for the Egyptian State Railways. (*GEC Traction*)

would be inadequate in winter working the engine is automatically speeded up to 620rpm when the heating load is switched on. Duplicate 40-cell lead-acid batteries of 92amp/hr capacity are provided on each motor coach, one for lighting and one for engine starting, though if required in emergency the two can be run in parallel. There is thus no problem with engine starting and the engines can be shut down as soon as the train has stopped at a terminus and restarted just a few minutes before departure.

The first 6-car set was completed in February 1957 and on the 25th of that month ran the $111\frac{1}{2}$ miles from Waterloo to Bournemouth West in 120 minutes with a three minute stop at Bournemouth Central. The first seven 6-car train sets which had 58ft 0in bodies on 56ft 11in underframes were completed by May, intended for a service to commence on 9 June 1957. However, a fire at Cannon Street station signalbox put the station out of action until an emergency signal frame was installed and four of the sets were commissioned from 6 May to operate as two 12-coach formations for peak hour commuter traffic.

In addition to the original seven sets, a further sixteen sets built on 63ft 5in underframes were needed to complete the total dieselisation of the Hastings service. By 17 June 1957 the first stage was introduced with ten sets, the original seven and three of the second consignment. The full service was implemented on 9 June 1958, with each unit then running an annual mileage of just over 90,000. This was comparable with

the Region's multiple-unit electric stock and considerably better than many main line locomotives.

These 23 sets were made up of seven sets with short bodied stock (58ft 0in) Nos 1001/7, nine sets of the longer stock (64ft 6in) Nos 1011/19, and seven buffet car sets Nos 1031/7. The flat sides of the narrow bodies were quite distinctive. The first-class seats were in compartments and the rest were of the open saloon type. The ride was not particularly good especially in the motor cars, but the services were an improvement on the previous steam-operated ones.

The service operated with 12-car trains semi-fast (six stops) to Tunbridge Wells where the trains were divided. Six cars ran on to Hastings with four stops and the other six cars followed a short while later as stopping trains (ten stops) to Hastings. In the up direction the process was reversed, with the two sets coupling at Tunbridge Wells. It was a regular hourly service leaving London (Charing Cross) at 20 minutes past each hour and leaving Hastings on the hour for the stopping train and 20 minutes past for the fast. There were also some fast buffet car trains to and from Cannon Street in the rush hours and which did not divide at Tunbridge Wells.

The service went into action with very little teething troubles, though there had been some failures of fuel injection pumps during the weeks of trial running — when these were changed from Bryce to CAV the problems were overcome. During the first three years there was only one serious engine failure, which was due to water from a porous cylinder head diluting the lubricating oil and causing damage to the bearings and crankshaft.

There were several complaints of noise, largely due

to the novelty of the diesel roar in a rural setting, but the turbocharger whistle almost amounting to a jet scream on these engines was particularly objectionable to some people; it was the same turbocharger as used on the engines in the Class 20 and Class 40 main line locomotives, which had not been the cause of any complaints. This problem was overcome by fitting a resonance silencer, which reduced the noise level from 94 to 90 decibels. These figures compare with 89 decibels for a steam suburban train, with 93 for an express steam freight and 77 for an electric train.

Early on, the bogie side frames were noted to be developing cracks in the bottom solebar, and they were reinforced by additional rivetted plates and extra vertical webs. Those repairs were carried out at the special maintenance depot which had been set up at St Leonard's, West Marina. This included a carriage shed 750ft long by 85ft with five tracks, two 23,500-gallon fuel tanks with bund wall surround, and four road inspection shed 440ft long by 85ft wide. A 25-ton overhead travelling crane spans two of the tracks at the closed end of the shed to enable engines and bogies to be changed. The engine change can be completed in eight hours. The engine and generator set is then sent to the main works at Eastleigh for overhaul, travelling on a special 13-ton four-wheel flat wagon fitted with vacuum brakes. Four of these wagons were built, as they are also used for the similar power units fitted in Class 73 electro-diesel locomotives.

When a train set arrived at the depot it was first passed through an automatic carriage-washing machine and then to the fuelling point, 20 minutes being allowed for each operation. Afterwards if any maintenance was required it went to the inspection shed, but if not it went to the carriage shed for cleaning; it had been found desirable to keep the two processes quite separate because of the different types of fluids involved.

The daily examination, which involves checking for leaks and topping-up water and oil levels, is carried out in the carriage shed. The other monthly, 3-monthly and 6-monthly examinations are completed in the inspection shed. Bogies are removed for tyre turning at 80,000 miles and the power units were exchanged after 7,500 hours, corresponding roughly to 180,000 miles; this figure has now gone up to 10,000 hours. The tyre turning and engine change periods did not co-incide since the timing was adjusted in order to obtain the maximum use from each component between changes.

At Eastleigh the engines are dismantled, chemically cleaned and all wearing parts such as bearings, cylinder liners and piston rings measured and recorded. Cylinder heads are hydraulically tested to 30lb/sq in and valves re-faced at an angle of 45deg 15min with the valve seat ground to 45deg.

During early overhauls it was noted that wear on the valve guides had caused the valve heads to damage the top of the cylinder liners, and this was found to be due to low oil temperature caused by defective thermostats.

The original bi-metal thermostats were then replaced by a wax-cell type with greater operating potential, which cured this trouble. Some slight cracks in the piston crowns were found to be due to the use of a wrong alloy and these were changed to a revised formula. The other most troublesome feature was the movement of turbine blades in the turbocharger due to creep in the lacing wire — this was overcome by splitting the lacing wire into three sections. These engines on the Hastings service were operating at an overall load factor of 45.5 percent on the stopping trains and the miles per engine hour came to just over 39. In 1960 Mr W. J. A. Sykes, the chief mechanical and electrical engineer of the Southern Region gave a paper to the Institution of Locomotive Engineers in which he described the performance of the engines as highly satisfactory.

Before the Hastings buffet car sets were delivered a batch of eighteen 2-car sets was built for the Hampshire lines, as recommended in the 1951 Bowles Report. These sets, numbered 1101–1118, were originally fitted with the 500hp engine. They were followed by four more 500hp 2-car sets, Nos 1119–1122, for East Sussex. The next batch was consignment of 3-car units for Hampshire, and in order to meet the schedules with the extra trailer the engines were uprated to 600hp. This was achieved by the use of the larger Napier MS200 turbocharger in place of the TS100 used on the original engines, and by an alteration in the fuel pump settings.

There was some controversy over these ratings, as they were agreed to by the engine makers on the understanding the maximum output would only be used for a few minutes during acceleration. Once a driver has the extra power available he uses it regardless, and this soon showed up in extensive piston fatigue due to the additional heating of the piston crown. These engines should have been fitted with an intercooler at the higher rating, but the Southern Region did not want the complication of an extra cooling circuit and the increased weight involved. The change in piston material which was required by the cracking in the early days helped to lessen this problem but piston life on the 600hp engines was always limited by this feature to around 10,000 hours. When the original eighteen 2-car sets in Hampshire were provided with an extra trailer they were likewise fitted with the 600hp engines which had originally been supplied for the second batch of thirteen 6-car trains for the Hastings line. These 26 engines were divided into 22 for Hampshire and four for East Sussex, while the 500hp engines displaced were used on the Hastings main line stock.

In 1962 a further twenty-six 3-car sets were commissioned, seven for the Reading to Portsmouth service and nineteen for the Oxted and East Sussex lines, to work between Victoria and East Grinstead, Tunbridge Wells and Brighton via Uckfield.

The Oxted line sets had side doors to each bay or

Southern Region Class 201 diesel-electric 6-car unit with 56ft 11in long coaches, for the Hastings line, at Sevenoaks in 1957. The unit is in all-over green livery, before the introduction of yellow warning panels on the front. (*English Electric*)

Class 201 Hastings line diesel-electric unit, in BR blue-and-grey livery, with full yellow end. The fourth car, originally all first-class, has been partially de-classified. (*British Rail*)

compartment like the other 2- and 3-car units, but were built with 8ft 6in wide bodies instead of the 9ft of the other units because of restricted clearances in the tunnels at Tunbridge Wells, slightly less restrictive than Mountfield tunnel on the Tonbridge–Hastings line. First class and toilets were in the centre trailer instead of the driving trailer.

By this time the DEMU fleet included twenty 6-car sets and fifty-eight 2-car or 3-car sets making a total of 98 power cars. The number of steam locomotives in the Region was 621 at the beginning of that year.

Just as these services were getting established and showing good results (the Hastings line resulted in an increase in passengers of 40 percent by 1960 compared with 1956) the Beeching Plan was unleashed which threatened several of the services worked by these DEMU railcar sets. They included Ashford-Hastings, Ashford–New Romney, Crowhurst–Bexhill West, Three Bridges–Tunbridge Wells West, Tonbridge–Brighton, Tonbridge–Eastbourne, Brighton–Horsham, Guildford–Horsham, Winchester–Alton, Portsmouth–Andover, Romsey–Andover, and Reading–Tonbridge. Stations intended for closure included Crowhurst, Edenbridge, Frant and Wadhurst. The stations named were reprieved as well as some of the proposed branch lines, but the closure of the line between Uckfield and Lewes meant that the 19 Oxted line sets which were maintained at St Leonard's had to make a 100-mile detour by way of East Croydon and Lewes in order to get there and back; they were too wide to work over the Tonbridge to St Leonards section and the line between Eridge and Polegate (the Cuckoo Line) had also been closed.

In 1964 three of the original 6-car Hastings sets, Nos 1002/3/4 were withdrawn and the six power cars with one each of the trailer seconds were coupled to a 64ft 0in ex-electric driving trailer 9ft 0in wide. These re-established six sets numbered 1201–1206 went into use on a new service between Reading and Tonbridge via Redhill. Because of the mixed stock widths these were known as 'Tadpole' sets and became Class 206.

The classes of this stock at that stage were:—

Class	Type	No of sets
201	6-car Hastings short stock	4
202	6-car Hastings 64ft 6in stock	11
203	6-car Hastings Buffet car stock	5
40 500hp Power Units		
204	2-car East Sussex stock	4
205	3-car Hampshire & Berkshire stock	29
206	3-car Reading–Tonbridge stock (Tadpole)	6
207	3-car Oxted Line stock	19
58 600hp Power Units		

During the next few years some problems arose in operation, although these were remarkably few. Some

cylinder blocks were found to be cracked due to core shift, and a change in water treatment showed up some cracks at the base of the cylinder liners that had previously been conveniently blocked up with sludge. The 4-cylinder version of this engine was dropped from the manufacturer's production, making spares difficult and expensive. This resulted in the Southern Region buying some engines from the Ministry of Defence for spares and replacements; as these engines had only been used for standby sets they were in almost new condition. The current method of water treatment for these units is to use soluble oil in the summer and an inhibited anti-freeze in the winter.

The governors on these engines were of the 4-step electro-magnetic type as opposed to the pneumatically-controlled type used on the main line locomotives. This was because air control was not desirable over a 12-car train due the pressure drop in that length of pipe. In order to permit better acceleration with this manual notching system the governors were modified to limit the rate of change of engine speed to prevent the overloads tripping out. The driver could move straight to full power on his controller as on an electric multiple unit.

One unusual problem showed up in the sets operating between Hastings and Ashford across the once dreaded Romney Marsh, where the amount of sheeps' wool blowing about found its way onto the radiator matrix and formed a base for oil and brake block dust to coagulate into an almost solid mixture. This presented quite a cleaning problem and entailed the use of steam jets to remove the blockage.

Some figures for operating costs had been given by W. J. A. Sykes in his paper to the Institution of Locomotive Engineers for 1959 and these worked out at 8.4d (3.5p) per car mile which included fuel, maintenance and renewal provision. Figures quoted for 1977 give the equivalent costs as 21.4p per mile. Allowing for the inflation during that period which is 350 percent, the figure of 8.4d would by 1977 come to 12.2p. The main differences are accounted for by increased costs in main works (overhauls) and in the renewal provision. The estimated cost replacement 3-car sets (Class 210) in 1977 being £450,000.

From 1976 two buffet cars were withdrawn from the Hastings sets and one of these was converted for use as the Southern Region general manager's saloon. The other was fitted with APT bogies and used as a tilt testing car along with the APT-POP space frame units.

During 1963 Hampshire unit No 1129 had been fitted with a Dorman 12QT engine which was rated for this duty at 725hp at 1,500rpm. Being a 12-cylinder engine this gave a much smoother ride in the power car, but the engine did not prove satisfactory in service largely due to troubles with the cams and valve gear, and it was soon replaced by its original reliable 4-cylinder 4SRKT unit. This engine was tried out since its designed rating was 910hp and there was a proposal to introduce a 900hp 4-car set for use on a service

Class 205 (3H) unit at London Bridge. The leading two vehicles are identical in body style to equivalent SR electric stock, except that the diesel driving trailer composites have only two first class compartments instead of three. (*British Rail*)

Class 207 (3D) unit with 8ft 6in wide bodies at London Bridge. The first-class and toilet accommodation is in the centre trailer. Note also the later style of cab end, without overhanging roof, with smaller indicator panel, and pockets for jumper cables. (Compare with the Class 205 unit). The black triangle is painted on the end of the car that houses the guard's compartment – this is also done on Southern Region EMUs. (*British Rail*)

between Brighton and Cardiff. Proposals for these sets also included a 6-cylinder version of the English Electric RKT range, but this would have been overweight. Consideration was also given to the use of an underfloor AEC engine at 230hp and the flat Paxman 450hp type that had been tried out by Derby in 1958. Eventually this whole project was dropped.

The Hastings 6-car units have found their way to many parts of the rail system particularly as specials for clubs and outings because of an absence of limitations on their narrow bodies. In 1968 one of the Hastings sets was tried out on the East Coast line to Doncaster for ride qualities following the serious accident at Hither Green on the 5 November 1967, as a result of which no fault was attached to the train for the accident. Specials have worked as far away as Spalding and Paignton, which is probably their furthest run from London. For some years these units were employed on the Brighton–Exeter through service.

In 1980 set No 1033 was involved in an accident at Appledore and motor car No 60036 was written-off. In that year the remaining buffet cars were withdrawn from the Hastings service since the staff often outnumbered the customers during the daytime off-peak runs. In 1979 the Class 206 'Tadpole' sets were withdrawn and their service was replaced by Western Region Class 117 Pressed Steel DMUs, which then worked from Reading to Tonbridge and to Gatwick Airport. The trailers from the 'Tadpoles' were added to sets Nos 1103/4 and 1121/2 to form units 1401/4, now in Class 204.

As this book went to press a question mark hung over the future of the Hastings line 6-car units. The bodywork on these sets is only just being kept going by welding fresh strips along the lower panels, and cracks in the engine crankcases present an ever increasing problem. Authority was given in 1983 to electrify the line between Tonbridge and Bo-Peep Junction, St Leonards, which involves singling the track through the tunnels with limited clearances and resignalling. This would allow standard width electric stock to be used on the line; indeed the Southern hopes to operate services without acquiring new rolling stock by tighter rostering and transfers of electric stock from other areas made redundant by service reductions.

Class 210 Diesel-Electric Trains

The broad specification for the Class 210 stock was similar to the Class 313 dual voltage electric trains used on the Eastern Region between London (Moorgate) and Welwyn Garden City. They were the first of the new generation of EMUs based on the MkIII passenger coaches produced in 1976. Since it was intended that the DEMU stock should be able to operate in multiple with electric stock this entailed around 1,100hp of installed diesel engine output. As this stock had to have gangway connections at both

ends a through passageway was necessary past the power unit, which entailed a small high-speed engine. It was unfortunate that the previous 4SRKT engine was no longer available, since that could now have given over 1100hp at its current rating, but it would have posed problems over weight and passenger access.

Class 210 is designed for a maximum speed of 90mph (145kph). It is provided with Tightlock couplers and with power and braking systems compatible with the electric stock with which it may have to work. Two types of unit have so far been built: No 210.002 is a 3-car set providing 203 third-class seats, and is fitted with an MTU 12-cylinder diesel engine type 12V 396 TC12 rated at 1,225hp (915kW) at 1,500rpm, driving a GEC alternator. The other set is No 210.001, a 4-car unit providing 232 seats including 22 first-class, and toilet facilities. This set is fitted with a 6-cylinder Paxman Valenta engine type 6RP 200 producing 1,125hp (839kW) at 1,500rpm, driving a Brush alternator. Both alternators produce 780kW at 1200 volts 3-phase which is rectified to feed four traction motors each rated at 190kW, capable of giving a maximum tractive effort of 20,800lb (92kN).

The controller has five notches from idling at 750rpm up to full speed at 1,500rpm, and a load regulator controls the main alternator excitation through thyristors to achieve the engine speed selected at normal full position of the fuel rack.

The auxiliary alternator produces 3-phase alternating current at variable voltage from 207 volts to 415 volts to supply the heaters, the compressor, and fan motors. A rectified supply from this source also supplies dc at 110volts for batteries, lighting, controls and public address systems, there is one battery of 217amp/hr capacity for lighting, controls and starting, unlike the Southern units where the two battery system proved so effective.

Heating is by a combination of pressure ventilation which absorbs 17kW and convector heaters under the seat with a rating of 8kW. The body structure is insulated by 50mm of glass fibre matting and the windows are double-glazed, but the heating has to cope with sliding doors, two to each side of the coach, which can be operated by passengers as well as by the guard. An electrically-driven compressor is mounted under the power car to supply air for braking and for the secondary bogie suspension as well as the sliding doors. There are disc brakes on all wheels, controlled through a Westcode three-step electro-pneumatic system.

The power car bogies are a new type, BP20, designed for a 19-tonne axle load, with a wheelbase of 2,710mm (107in) and weigh 11.4 tonnes including the traction motors. The primary suspension is by Clouth rubber springs with hydraulic dampers, and the secondary suspension consists of air springs which provide freedom of movement of the body in all directions. The body height is monitored and the air pressure to the springs varied to suit. The disc brake calipers are bolted on to the side frames adjacent to each wheel and each of the actuators contains a spring-applied and air-released parking brake.

The trailer car bogies are of the BT13 type, similar to the BX1 type used for many EMU vehicles; the primary suspension is by chevron rubber springs above the axleboxes, with trailing arm registration. The secondary suspension is similar to that on the BP20 bogies. These bogies have proved satisfactory in service, but the dampers on the BP20 bogies are still in need of some improvement.

Access for engine maintenance is through doors in the passageway past the power unit, and all the components requiring attention are supposed to be on that side of the engine. The sequence of depot attention is intended to be as shown below.

The two Class 210 sets were used on extensive trials on the Western Region working out of Paddington to Slough and Didcot and were later moved to other routes.

It is clear, though, that the Class 210 is not really the answer for the future; as built it is too expensive and too complex for the sort of services it was intended for and it is unlikely to see extensive series production. Indeed as described in Chapter 4 the BRB is again looking at underfloor-engined units for the future.

Class 210 servicing programme

Nightly:	Fuelling and checking brakes.
Weekly:	A Examination. Water and oil levels.
	Measure brake pad thickness.
2-Monthly:	B Examination. Water and oil sampling.
	Inspection of all operating gear on the train.
4-monthly:	C Examination.
Yearly:	D Examination.
2-yearly:	E Examination.
4-yearly:	Main works examination and overhaul.

6 The Blue Pullmans

It is not entirely clear how the concept for the luxury diesel Pullman trains which entered service in 1960 came about, for they were so totally different from anything that had run on BR before. True there had been a multiple-unit Pullman before, the all-electric Brighton Belle which began in 1933, but essentially the three Belle units were little more than conventional Pullman cars of the time marshalled as five car sets with a motor coach at each end which included a driver's cab and carried the traction equipment. The diesel Pullmans of 1960 were so much more luxurious than other Pullmans of the day, even superior to other new locomotive-hauled Pullmans which entered service on the East Coast at about the same time. For a start the diesel Pullmans had streamlined power cars at each end with the fronts sloped sharply back to blend with roof and bodyside. Second, each set was finished in a striking new blue and white livery unlike the normal Pullman umber and cream. Third, internally the units were fully air conditioned, the first coaches for public service to be so fitted on BR, with high standards of sound and thermal insulation, fixed double-glazed windows wall to wall carpeting and modern pattern seats and tables styled by industrial designers.

A number of factors influenced the decision by BR to produce this small number of luxury trains. One was the need to provide alternative services between London and Birmingham, and Manchester while the main line from Euston was disorganised by electrification and rebuilding work during the early 1960s — which it was hoped would be filled by the luxury Pullmans in wooing businessmen to the alternative routes, and second was the Trans Europ Express concept of fast first class only luxury daytime trains on international routes, which had been developed across Western Europe during the 1950s to combat air travel. Undoubtedly the influence of Dr F. Q. den Hollander, former President of Netherlands Railways who was involved in the planning of the TEE network and who in 1954 was a member of the Technical Research Committee of BR, helped to boost the BR Blue Pullman project.

During the mid 1950s the government of the day had approved the roundly £1,200 million investment in the 1955 modernisation plan which included an amount of £345 million on the replacement of steam traction and £285 million for new coaches and diesel multiple unit vehicles.

In June 1955 some comments by the Technical Development and Research Committee on modernisation plans included the following:

1. Do not let the existing vacuum-braked vehicles impede the implementation of air brakes. This was objected to by the Regional Managers and supported by the BR Management, which ruled in favour of the vacuum brake in February 1956.
2. If DMU trains prove more effective in service do not adhere to locomotive haulage.
3. Do not let steam heating hold back the adoption of electric heating for new stock.

All of these recommendations were taken into account in the decision to build the high-speed Blue Pullman trains since they were air-braked multiple-units, with electric ancillaries including heating.

Dr den Hollander had also been connected with the Dutch firm of Werkspoor whose RUB range were the only Dutch-built diesel engines suitable for main line rail traction. Since the Dutch railway system was almost entirely electrified there was not much home market potential for these engines. Werkspoor accordingly formed an association with SIG of Switzerland to build some diesel-electric trains which were suitable for widespread European duties, as part of the Trans Europ Express train concept. These were to be of a high power to weight ratio, of luxury standards and to avoid delays at frontier crossings with customs examination on board. The intention was that many of the important European business centres could be covered for a return journey in the same day, to compete with air travel. All seats had to be reserved in advance, dining facilities were provided and the trains were first class only with a supplement.

The initial reason for building these trains as self-contained diesel units was because in the mid 1950s there were gaps in electrification which meant that steam or diesel traction had to be used on ordinary services where there was no catenary.

Moreover even where lines *were* electrified, different countries used different electrification systems, 3000V dc in Italy and Belgium, 1500V dc in the Netherlands and France (the Paris, Dijon route to Marseilles) 15,000V 16⅔ Hz ac in Switzerland and Germany (also Austria although it was not involved in the TEE concept) and 25kV 50 Hz ac in France (Paris–Strasbourg and Thionville–Basel although electrification on these routes had not been completed when the TEE concept started). Multi-voltage traction units were not developed until the early 1960s.

The first of the diesel TEE trains were the Dutch/Swiss 4-car units, one car of which was the power car containing two 1000hp Werkspoor engines for traction and one 800hp set for air-conditioning, cooking, lighting and other auxiliaries. Five sets were built and provided services between Paris–Amsterdam and Amsterdam–Zurich. French two-car TEE units provided services between Paris, Brussels and Amsterdam, and Lyons and Milan while German streamlined sets with five intermediate cars and power cars equipped with 1000hp Maybach diesel engines started services between Paris–Dortmund, Ostend–Dortmund and Hamburg–Zurich.

A wooden model of the Dutch/Swiss train was shown to some BTC personnel in 1955. In March 1957 following the relaxation in fuel oil restrictions enquiries were put out for five new high-speed Pullman trains in two versions: two 6-car all first-class sets for the London Midland Region and three 8-car sets two class for the Western Region. There was also a proposition to run either a 6-car or an 8-car set on the former Great Central line, to form the Master Cutler which then was still running on that line. This would have entailed a timing of 170 minutes between Marylebone and Sheffield. Since most of the route was limited to 80mph, that would have given a saving of over one hour, but in 1958 the Master Cutler service was transferred to the Kings Cross route where it did the journey in 165 minutes, and the Great Central line Pullman idea was dropped. The Master Cutler was later transferred to the St Pancras line, where with haulage by a Class 40 diesel it reached Sheffield in 150 minutes with stops at Leicester and Chesterfield.

It was appropriate that the first of these new Pullman trains completed late in 1959 should go into service on the former Midland main line between St Pancras and Manchester, since it was on the Midland Railway that in 1874 James Allport commenced the operation of the first Pullman cars in the UK. Those coaches were a novelty and so were the Blue Pullmans, the latter being the first fully air-conditioned stock to operate on British Rail. The trains were described in publicity by their builders, Metropolitan Cammell Carriage & Wagon Company of Saltley, Birmingham, as Luxury Travel and The Way Ahead.

The two power cars in each train were each fitted with a turbocharged MAN diesel engine type L12V18/21S having twelve cylinders 180mm bore by 210mm stroke and running at 1,445rpm driving a 650kW GEC generator having a lap wound armature. The engine, which was similar to those fitted in the Class 21 locomotives, was equipped with a Napier turbocharger and an Ardleigh 7-step governor — though supplied by the North British Locomotive Company all ten engines were built in Germany by MAN. The output from the generator was supplied to four 4-pole GEC traction motors with a rating of 199hp, mounted two in the rear bogie of the power car

and two in the leading bogie of the adjoining trailer coach. The motors were fully spring-borne and mounted in bogies of the Swiss Schlieren design built by Metro-Cammell. These were the first fully spring-borne traction motors to be used in diesel-powered stock, though similar ones had been used in the Swiss Brown-Boveri gas turbine locomotive No 18000 built for the WR. Overhung from the main generator was an auxiliary generator rated at 10kW and supplying 110volts to the starter batteries and the control circuits. The whole power unit was mounted on Matalastik anti-vibration mountings. The cooling group, placed between the engine and the driver's cab, consisted of two vertical radiators in the bodyside with a 45in roof-mounted extractor fan driven by a Serck-Behr hydrostatic motor.

The 6-coach sets for the London Midland Region were made up of two power cars (Type 1) with 12 first-class seats, two kitchen cars (Type 4) with 18 seats, and two parlour cars (Type 6) with 36 seats, making 132 first-class seats in all. The 8-coach sets for the Western Region comprised two power cars (Type 2) with 18 second-class seats, two parlour cars (Type 3) with 42 second-class seats, two kitchen cars (Type 5) with 18 first-class seats and two parlour cars (Type 6) with 36 first-class seats, making a total of 108 first-class and 120 second-class. The 6-car sets were 409ft long and weighed 299 tons, while the 8-car sets were 545ft long and weighed 364 tons.

All the passenger accommodation was in open saloons, traditional to the Pullman name since the first Midland Railway versions, though not popular with the conservative British in 1874. All the seating was in new pattern airline style seats with deep foam cushions and upholstered in red or blue striped fabric contrasting with the traditional Pullman individual armchairs. The seats in the first-class were also reclinable. Fixed tables were provided at all seats. The decor was of rosewood and ebony veneers with plastics to the bodyside walls up to the luggage racks. Windows were double-glazed with adjustable venetian blinds between the panes of glass. A high level of sound insulation was achieved by asbestos insulation, and carpeted insulated floors.

All cars were air-conditioned by Stone's roof-mounted units and the heating was at floor level. Temperature levels could be set at 68°, 71° or 74° farenheit and maintained by the use of electric heaters or a refrigeration system using Freon 12. Power supplies for the air-conditioning, the lighting and the kitchens were provided by two underfloor mounted Rolls-Royce 180hp 8-cylinder diesel alternators. Those in the 6-car sets were under the kitchen cars, under which was also one of the power bogies, and those in the 8-car sets were under the second-class parlour car, which also had a power bogie. The Stone's Tonum alternator provided 133kVA at 400volts 3-phase 50Hz. Normally one set was sufficient to provide the necessary power for its complete train, but the two

The German TEE – a front-end view. (*DB*)

might be required in extreme conditions. A shore power supply was also provided at terminal stations and depots on the routes served by these trains to save running the generators during layover periods.

Braking was by compressed air using the Westinghouse electro-pneumatic system featuring a high speed control. The driver's brake valve had six positions:-

Position 1   Release and running.
Position 2   Full service application.
Position 3   Lap.
Position 4   Service.
Position 5   Emergency.
Position 6   Shut down.

The main air reservoir pressure was maintained at 125lb/sq in by electrically-driven compressors, one under each power car; the brake line pressure was kept at 70lb/sq in. The high-speed feature was actuated by a

MAN 12-cylinder 1,000hp engine and generator, as fitted in the Blue Pullman units. (*GEC Traction*)

tacho-generator which energised a special magnet valve on each vehicle at speeds in excess of 40mph and cut out below 30mph on falling speeds.

The trains were arranged so that they could be divided into two identical half sets for maintenance and repair, but the coupling system and special gangways designed by the Schweizerische Industrie Gesellschaft took so long to disconnect that the trains were never split. This meant that one complete train had to be held in reserve in each of the Regions, thus making the whole exercise very unremunerative.

Each kitchen car, which served its own half of the train set, included a pantry with refrigerator, stainless-steel sink, sterilizer, Ascot water heater and extraction fan. In the kitchen itself was another refrigerator with deep-freeze capacity, a sink unit with Ascot water heater, a double gas stove with eye-level grill fuelled by Calor gas and complemented by a hot cupboard and an extraction fan, all in a space less than 17ft by 6ft. Each kitchen could be expected to produce 66 meals in the case of the Midland Region and 114 in the Western Region sets.

The driver's cabs at the end of each set were well laid out with two adjustable seats and the usual master controller, brake controls and instruments. There were special indicator lights for the high-speed brake, as well as a test button for fault location and a deadman's treadle. An automatic warning system was installed as well as a Loudaphone for communication with the guard, though the latter was for essential conversations affecting the working of the train and to be used only in emergency when in motion. The riding in the cab was as good as anywhere in the train, and considerably better than in most diesel locomotives as experienced by the author in a ride from Paddington to Leamington on one occasion.

The guard's compartment in each power car was equipped with a microphone connected to a public address system in each car and announcements could be made either by the guard or by the Pullman car conductor.

The exterior was finished in a Nanking blue with a broad white band enclosing the windowed section along the sides of each car. Each power car had a rounded nose with a white band enclosing the windscreens, and the Pullman crest in the centre above the marker lights. These trains were not provided with 4-character headcode panels of contemporary locomotives, but had three panel-lights just above the buffers. They were used to denote a Class 1 passenger working by two white discs or lights, one over each buffer, or empty carriage working by one light over the right-hand buffer and one in the centre.

The roofs were finished in light grey, the underframes in aluminium and the bogies in black. A draw hook was provided at each end of the train for haulage by locomotives in an emergency and standard oval buffers were also fitted. There was no provision for towing additional vehicles; originally the train sets could not be coupled together for multiple operation though this equipment was fitted later.

The first pair of 6-car train sets for the London Midland Region were ready by September 1959 and

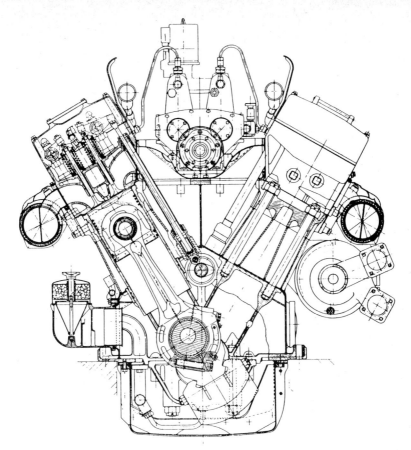

Cross-section of the MAN L12V 18/21 engine.

after a short trial on the line to Walsall were tried out on the Eastern Region pending settlement of some staffing problems on the LM Region. As Pullman cars had not been operated on the LM Region since the Midland cars, the restaurant car staff feared a relegation to less remunerative services or even redundancy if Pullman Car staff were used. A strike of restaurant car crews delayed the start of the Blue

Pullman service, intended for November 1959, until 4 July 1960. The problem was overcome by using LMR dining car staff kitted out with Pullman style uniforms, which were also used for a number of top flight non-Pullman services. The LM staff were trained in Pullman style service which differed in detail from conventional restaurant cars. In some ways the delay was a blessing in that it enabled a crucial operating problem to be at least partially overcome in time for the opening runs.

That concerned the riding of the power bogies, one under the rear end of the power car and the other under the next trailer car. The bogies of Schlieren design and built by Metro-Cammell, incorporated

Parlour car for the London Midland 6-car version of the Blue Pullman units. (*Metro-Cammell*)

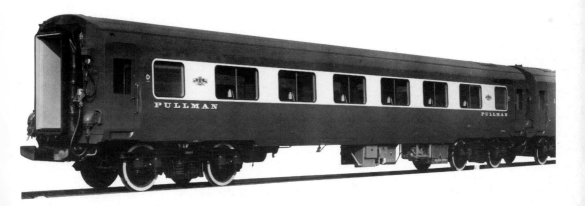

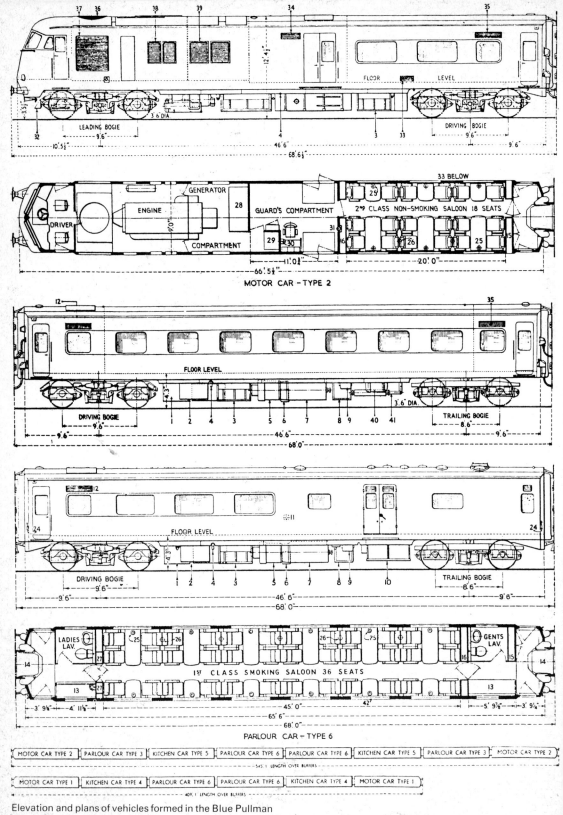

Elevation and plans of vehicles formed in the Blue Pullman
units: from top to bottom – Power car first type 1 (six car),
power car second type 2 (eight car), parlour second type 3
(eight car), kitchen parlour first type 4 (six car), parlour first
type 6. Bottom, formation of eight and six-car trains.

Interior of second class saloon in 8-car Western Region
Blue Pullman unit. (*Metro-Cammell*)

Front end of Western Region Blue Pullman power car No
W60096. (*Metro-Cammell*)

damped helical coiled springs, and the traction motors were fully spring-borne in order to reduce the unsprung weight to a minimum. The drive from the motor gears was through a Brown Boveri spring drive unit with the drive at opposite ends in the case of each axle. This meant that the total spring damping effect was greater at one end of each axle than at the other end, and this effect was in a diagonal plane across each bogie. This caused some very erratic riding, particularly in the passenger end of the power cars. Although this was partially overcome by increasing the damping at the other end of each driven axle, the ride was never as good as had been anticipated when these bogies were specified. The effect was made worse by the vertical-striped seating upholstery, which was rather trying to the eyes when the riding was particularly poor.

A demonstration run with one of the 8-car sets was made on 24 June 1960 between Marylebone and High Wycombe, during which speeds of up to 90mph were attained. This run was for the benefit of 100 representatives of foreign governments and overseas railways, who commented favourably on the decor and on the smoothness of acceleration and braking. On 1 July an inaugural run was made on the LM Region between St Pancras and Leicester — on that occasion 114 guests, nearly all from UK firms, both customers and suppliers were included.

The full service started on 4 July 1960. Leaving from Manchester (Central) at 08.50, the train ran the 190 miles to St Pancras in 193 minutes, arriving at 12.03. It then left St Pancras at 12.45 for Leicester, covering the 99 miles in 85 minutes, with a return from Leicester at 14.33 arriving at 16.00 hours. The last run left St Pancras at 18.10 and reached Manchester at 21.21 a journey time of 191 minutes. These times included a stop at Cheadle Heath in each direction, where a special car park was provided for commuters in that part of Manchester. The 182 miles between St Pancras and Cheadle Heath were run in 173 minutes each way. As a result of some adverse comments on the tardy arrival in London, the departure times were put forward in 1962 by one hour to give an arrival time at 11.00, thus allowing a full seven hours of business time in London. It was then proposed to extend the midday fill-in run to Nottingham. This caused further trouble for a couple of months with the restaurant car staff taking industrial action by returning to the kitchens between Leicester and Nottingham. To minimise inconvenience to passengers, a rota of Pullman clerical staff travelled on the train in order to allocate reserved seats on the run from Nottingham; the restaurant car staff re-appeared at Leicester and normal service was then resumed. These staffing problems prevented the use of the other set on the LM Region, though some of the locomotive-hauled Pullman cars were transferred from the Southern Region to act as a standby in case both the Blue Pullman sets did not manage to get into service. One cannot help feeling that a little prior consultation might have avoided some of these staff problems.

The Western Region was able to make better use of its three train sets and operated three services, the Bristol Pullman, the Birmingham Pullman and the South Wales Pullman. The last-named had been inaugurated with locomotive-hauled stock from 13 June 1955 and this stock was then used as standby for the other Blue Pullman sets. It was known irreverently as the Wells Fargo set!

The South Wales Pullman was based on Old Oak Common and worked the 08.50 from Paddington to Swansea stopping at Newport, Cardiff, Bridgend, Port Talbot and Neath. The timing was leisurely, with an allowance of 151 minutes for the 133.5 miles to Newport, although this was reduced to 145 minutes for the up train which left Swansea at 16.30. The supplementary Pullman fares at that time were 4s 0d (20p) second-class to Newport, 5s 0d (25p) to Port Talbot and Swansea, with first-class at 7s 0d (35p) and 10s 0d (50p) respectively. By comparison the second-class single to Newport in 1958 was £1 2s 4d (£1.12) and that to Swansea was £1 11s 10d (£1.59), −£2 7s 9d (£2.38) first-class, or 2d (1p) per mile. To be in line with inflation the fare to Newport should now be £7.90, but at the time of writing was £14.50.

The Bristol Pullman worked two services a day each way, leaving Bristol at 07.40 and 12.30, returning from Paddington at 10.05 and 16.55. This set was based on Dr Day's Sidings at Bristol.

The third set which worked the Birmingham Pullman was based at Cannock Road Sidings, Wolverhampton, and left that town for Paddington at 07.00 with stops at Birmingham (Snow Hill) and Leamington Spa. A midday turn to Birmingham left Paddington at 12.10, with the fastest timing of 84 minutes for the 87.2 miles to Leamington. The train then left Snow Hill at 14.30, with the day's final run from Paddington back to Wolverhampton at 16.50.

The daily runs for these services amounted to 382 miles for the South Wales Pullman, 466 miles for the Birmingham Pullman and 473 miles for the Bristol Pullman. The general reliability of the sets was remarkably good in view of the complexity of the equipment. The German-built MAN diesels gave much less trouble than their British-built counterparts, though they did suffer from the same basic troubles due to cylinder heads, combustion chambers and exhaust manifolds. They also benefitted by being rated at only 1,000hp against the 1100hp for the similar engines in the North British and Swindon built Type 2 locomotives; that extra 10 percent made all the difference in peak temperature of vital components such as exhaust valves and piston rings.

These trains were the first diesel-electric main line units to be operated by the Western Region, and it was to be a further three years before the Region received its first diesel-electric locomotive, Class 37 No D6819. This was why the schedules at first did not push the equipment too hard since there remained bad memories of failed traction motors in the Brown Boveri gas turbine locomotive No 18000. This was also the reason why these trains were not used on the hilly route to Plymouth. Although the 6-car sets on the London Midland Region had to cope with the 980ft ascent of the Peak Forest route between Derby and Manchester the balancing speed on those grades would have been around 50mph, but on the section between Newton Abbot and Plymouth it would have been down to 24mph, thus imposing too high a heating load on the traction motors.

The trains had the benefit of travelling technicians from the CM&E department and they had absolute priority for maintenance at the stabling points to the detriment of the other standard stock.

While the LM Region had set the pace in operating speeds by running the 99.1 miles to Leicester in 83 minutes at an average of 71.6mph, later speeding-up of the Bristol Pullman entailed running the 94 miles to Chippenham (the home of the Westinghouse Brake Company) in 73 minutes at an average speed of 77.3mph.

By the Spring of 1966 the electrification of the LM Region main line from Euston to Manchester together with the new MkII coaches had rendered the Midland Pullman superfluous, and with two sets involved at around £400,000 apiece the operation was completely uneconomic. There was a proposal to transfer the two sets to the Eastern Region, but the authorities wisely preferred to stick with their more flexible locomotive-hauled Pullman trains, so the two sets were transferred to the Western Region. There they were converted for two-class accommodation and arranged to run in multiple as a 12-car train for the popular early and late Bristol Pullman. In the midday period the train was split, with one half working to Bristol and the other to Oxford, but these midday workings were poorly patronised and were abandoned in 1969.

With the LM electrification complete to Birmingham in 1967 the Birmingham Pullman was no longer required and the set was transferred to the South Wales route to duplicate the morning and evening reverse workings. The original 8-car set used on the Bristol service and displaced by the new 12-car set became a spare since no other use could be found for it on the Western Region timetable.

In 1967 a new livery was adopted for the Pullman cars by then in BR ownership; this was a reversal of the original concept, with a dark blue band along the window areas and the rest in silver grey. The front end Pullman motif was also discarded. The Western Region 8-car set was the first to be re-painted in this livery, but the trains were only to have five years' operation in these colours as all were taken out of service in 1973. This was, according to one former Pullman executive, due to a wave of 'anti-Pullmanitis' engendered by a combination of the hotels department and the NUR.

During their last years the spare set was used for special excursions working into other Regions, and there was even a proposition to run a business-boosting train from Bristol to Paris via the Dover-Dunkerque ferry. This idea was welcomed by the SNCF, but had to be abandoned owing to the problems of dividing the train in order to get it onto the ferry.

Technically the Blue Pullmans could be considered a success story, but it is doubtful if their total cost (over £2 million) was ever justified. They set standards of comfort that were almost emulated in the stock designed for the HST and APT trains and it is a pity that one of the vehicles was not preserved. It was claimed that a large amount of blue asbestos in their insulation was a disadvantage, and it was believed to have caused problems in their final disposal.

Former Midland Pullman 6-car set working the WR's Bristol Pullman near Keynsham in 1968. (*P. J. Fowler*)

7 The HST Inter-City 125

The 95 sets of HST Inter-City 125 trains have undoubtedly given British Rail the finest and fastest fleet of diesel trains in the world. Though still not completely trouble-free the present level of operation has been achieved by patient development starting as far back as 1968.

In that year, which saw the demise of steam working on BR main lines, it was becoming obvious that a general speed-up of passenger services was needed in order to meet the competition from motorways and airlines. The electrification of the main line from Euston to Liverpool and Manchester had produced an increase in passenger journeys of 80 percent over the 1965 figure, and similar increases in speed were needed on the East Coast main line and on the Western Region, both of which then had no early prospect of electrification. Apart from the 22 Class 55 Deltics and the fifty Class 50s which could attain 100mph, none of the other main line diesels was built for more than 95mph and most of them for only 90mph. Trials with the Brush *Kestrel* 4,000hp locomotive which was designed for 125mph had proved abortive, because that speed could not be worked by reason of its high axle load and limited braking capacity. It was obvious that in order to handle a train of around 300 tons the full 4,000hp would be needed in order to run at the proposed speeds of 125mph (200kph) and that this could only be produced by a high-speed (1,500rpm) diesel engine.

Consideration was given the use of gas turbines, as was intended by the SNCF in France, but there was no suitable design comparable in cost with a diesel engine of the type proposed. This referred both to first cost and to running costs such as fuel and maintenance.

As far back as 1961 Metropolitan-Cammell, following the inauguration of its Blue Pullman trains, had put forward a proposal for a high-speed train in 6-car and 8-car formations, using underfloor engines. Each coach was to be equipped with two Rolls-Royce 238hp engines, making 2,856hp for the 6-car set and 3,808hp for the 8-car unit. Seating was proposed as 84 first-class and 172 second-class for the 6-car set and 84 first-class and 256 second-class for the 8-car set. With the power proposed the operating speed would not have been much more than the 105mph then occasionally obtainable on BR main lines and this would not have achieved the desired operational speeds.

In 1958 the English Electric Company had started the design of a high-speed diesel engine with a 7.75in cylinder bore and 8.5in stroke running at 1,500rpm, intended to produce 2,700hp from 12 cylinders, but in 1963 after spending just over £1 million this project was dropped just as one engine was due for trials in one of the 'Baby Deltics' Type 2 Bo-Bo locomotives on the ER. Two people who were concerned with this project in its early days were Walter Jowett of English Electric, who later went to BR at Derby, and Dr Ron Hughes who went to Davey Paxman at Colchester. There he re-designed the Ventura engine of the same bore and stroke as the intended English Electric engine and this was renamed the Valenta. This version was a radical new design with a much stronger crankcase and a larger crankshaft and bearing surfaces. Because of the receptive attitude of Mr T. C. B. Miller at BR who had followed the developments at both the English Electric and the Paxman diesel engine factories (now both in GEC Diesels) the high-speed engine was much more acceptable and so formed the basis of the High Speed Train, which was first proposed in a limited circulation Black Book in 1968.

At first there was some confusion at the BR Board, which thought that this was just a diesel-powered version of the APT which had been envisaged for several years, but eventually the confusion was sorted out and authority was given on 24 February 1969 to expend £800,000 on the construction of a prototype train. Since this concept was based on the proposed new MkIII coaching stock and the power equipment was based on conventional locomotive components involving no radical departure from existing experience, the prototype train was completed and ready for trials by June 1972. Unfortunately, as with the Blue Pullmans, there was a lack of liaison with staff over drivers' remuneration, and this held up the trial running for a whole year.

The cost of the prototype train included two power cars and nine standard MkIII coaches though the train concept was for seven passenger cars, including two catering vehicles. Each power car included a Paxman 12-cylinder Valenta diesel engine type 12RP200L delivering 2,250hp at 1,500rpm driving a Brush 12-pole main alternator giving 1,480kW and an auxiliary alternator giving 313kW, of which 33kW was for the engine auxiliaries and 280kW for the train services, which were supplied from one engine only.

The Valenta engines installed were of the 60 degree VEE type and represented the ultimate that could be obtained from an engine of that bore and stroke (7.75in by 8.5in or 197mm by 216mm, running at

Paxman 'Valenta' engine and Brush alternator for BR Inter-City 125 units. (*Paxman Diesels*)

1,500rpm) without going to the complications of 2-stage turbocharging. It was estimated that by 1970 an output of 4hp/sq in of piston area should be obtainable with single-stage turbochargers working at a pressure ratio of 3/1, and in fact this was obtained at a figure of 2.7/1. In order to withstand the increased firing pressures amounting to 2,000lb/sq in (138 bar), the crankcase was fabricated using Stress-relieved steel castings, with tie bolts between the cylinder banks at the top of the VEE. The loading on the crankshaft entailed an increase in the main journal diameter to 9in (230mm) which gave a high rubbing speed of 3,535ft/min (18m/s) and this was met by the use of tin-aluminium main bearings.

To allow the connecting rods to be removed with their pistons through the liner bore this imposed a limit of 5.5in (140mm) to the diameter of the big-end bearing pins. The connecting rods of fork-and-blade design with a flat-palm fork and an angled blade rod carried big-end bearings for the fork rod of aluminium tin with a maximum area load of 3,580lb/sq in (247 bar). The blade rod shell is lead bronze and oscillates on the large end block. The connecting rods are machined all over and nitrided. The bolts rely on bolt stretch for locking. The pistons are single piece aluminium alloy with 11 percent silicon Wellworthy W52) and an Alfin top ring insert. Steel cooling coils were considered, but the plain jet from the top of the

connecting rod was found capable of keeping the piston temperatures down to 260°C at the piston crown. The four cast-iron piston rings run in liners which are chrome plated internally and externally.

The cylinder heads of cast-iron have two inlet and two exhaust valves operated by push rods worked from a camshaft in the centre of the VEE between the two cylinder blocks. The inlet valves are of EN59 with chrome-flashed stems; the exhaust valves of 21–4N have sulphurised stems and are designed to run at up to 650°C with a hoop stress of 20 ton sq in. The critical area between the exhaust valves is cooled by drilled passages in the cylinder head and the maximum temperature is kept down to 320°C.

Unlike most locomotive engines, the Valenta is fitted with a water-cooled aluminium exhaust manifold. This has the disadvantage of requiring 7 percent larger radiator capacity and of reducing the turbocharger efficiency by about 1.5 percent, but the failures due to the expansion bellows which had to be used with an air-cooled manifold were 20 per 1,000 hours on test and this was reduced by the water cooled type to less than one per 1,000 hours; there was also a considerable reduction in the fire risk in service, which is important with an unattended engine at one end of the train.

The Napier SA–084 turbocharger has plain bearings and these are fed from the engine lubricating oil system, which eliminated the problems of constantly checking the oil levels in the turbocharger system. The 18mm Bryce fuel injection pumps, type FCCAR180M0603 are individual to each cylinder, and mounted on camboxes on the outside of each

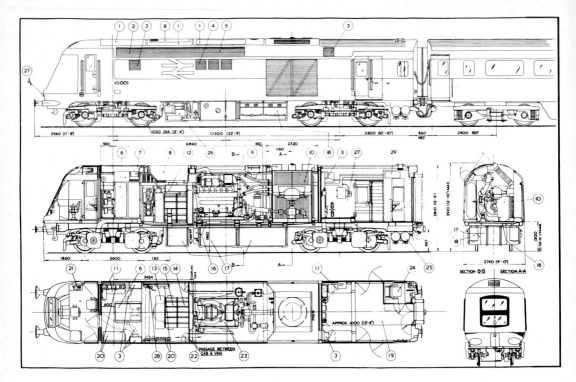

General arrangement diagram of power car for prototype HST – Car No 41001, Unit No 252.001. (*British Rail*)

cylinder bank with their own camshafts. They are designed to operate at a maximum fuel line pressure of 15,000lb/sqin. They were tested for 10,000 hours, half of which was at 17,000lb/sq in and at 10 percent above engine speed. Type NTDLB194HD462 injectors after considerable testing were found to give the best results, with ten holes of 0.36mm diameter at 150 degrees and with a sac size reduced to 1.8mm.

Since there were no dc windings on the main alternator this could not be used to start the engine, and separate starter motors were fitted similar to a standard automotive engine. These are fed from 110volt batteries mounted in boxes underneath the power cars.

The completed engine with all auxiliaries and with oil and water amounts to 17,402lb (7,891kg) and gives a specific figure of 7.7lb/hp. Prior to installation, both 12- and 16-cylinder versions of the engine were tested for the benefit of BR, the Admiralty and the Air Ministry, involving some 13,000 hours, of which the 12-cylinder version ran for over 7,000 hours.

The Brush alternator, flange-mounted to the engine casing, consists of two sets of twelve poles with rotating diodes on the end of the shaft for supplying dc to energise the rotating magnetic poles. The stator carries two corresponding windings, one to produce 1,500volts ac for traction and the other supplied 110volts for the engine auxiliaries and 850volts for the train supply, both these being rectified to dc. The Brush Electrical Engineering Company had for some years been supplying brushless alternators for use with

stationary diesel engines for normal power supplies and those designs were adapted for use in this application.

This arrangement of dc supplies was only used on the prototype train so as to be able to use standard MkIII coaches, but since the coaches on the production trains would not be used on any other trains the auxiliary supplies were arranged to be fed with alternating current.

The four traction motors for each power car were of the Brush type TMH 68–46, each of 467hp and permanently coupled in series parallel. Each was of the 4-pole type dc self-ventilated fully frame-suspended, with class H insulation on the armature windings and class F in the field windings. Frame suspension was necessary in order to reduce the unsprung weight to below 2.5 tons per axle stipulated by the civil engineer for 125mph operation. This involves a form of flexible drive, and instead of using the hollow shaft technique a different system was adopted by passing the drive shaft through the motor pinions and driving that through a flexible spider. This spider consists of 12 Twinflex links round a 340mm diameter disc which allows a 30mm rise and fall of the axle box in the bogie frame. The motor ratings are 467hp at 500 amps 1,425rpm continuous and 565 amps at 1,190rpm for one hour with a gear ratio of 2.5/1. With 40in (102mm) diameter wheels the continuous rating is at 68mph and the motor speed at 125mph is 2,620rpm.

The auxiliary alternator windings supply the starter battery and the other engine auxiliaries at 110volts controlled to within one percent; these include the control system, fuel and lubricating oil priming pumps,

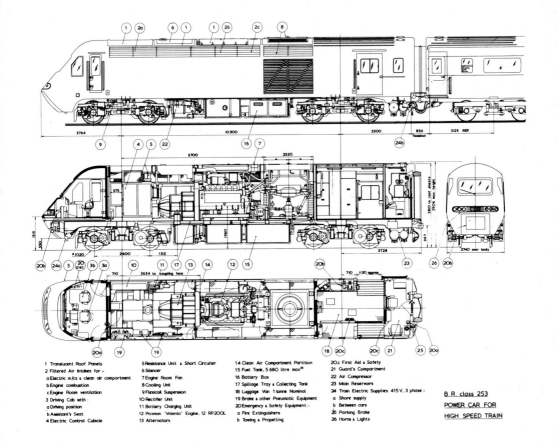

1 Translucent Roof Panels	5 Resistance Unit & Short Circuiter	14 Clean Air Compartment Partition	20c First Aid & Safety
2 Filtered Air Intakes for :-	6 Silencer	15 Fuel Tank, 5 680 litre max^m	21 Guard's Compartment
a Electric m/cs & clean air compartment	7 Engine Room Fan	16 Battery Box	22 Air Compressor
b Engine combustion	8 Cooling Unit	17 Spillage Tray & Collecting Tank	23 Main Reservoirs
c Engine Room ventilation	9 Flexicoil Suspension	18 Luggage Van 1 tonne Nominal	24 Train Electric Supplies 415 V, 3 phase :-
3 Driving Cab with :-	10 Rectifier Unit	19 Brake & other Pneumatic Equipment	a Shore supply
a Driving position	11 Battery Charging Unit	20 Emergency & Safety Equipment :-	b Between cars
b Assistant's Seat	12 Paxman "Valenta" Engine, 12 RP200L	a Fire Extinguishers	25 Parking Brake
4 Electric Control Cubicle	13 Alternators	b Towing & Propelling	26 Horns & Lights

B.R. class 253
POWER CAR FOR
HIGH SPEED TRAIN

General arrangement diagram for HST production power cars, Nos 43002 (Unit 253.001) onward. (*British Rail*)

but not the cooling group which consists of a Voith variable-speed mechanically-driven fan, activated from the free end of the engine and controlled through a hydrodynamic coupling in the hub of the fan impellor. The fan speed is determined by two thermostats, one in the primary cooling circuit, leaving the engine and the other in the secondary circuit entering the charge cooler. The fan diameter is 1,120mm (44in) absorbing 155hp at its full speed of 1,780rpm, the total heat dissipation being 1,060,000k cal/hour.

The power car body is generally similar to the MkIII coaches in the train, but special supports for the roof allow openings for the removal of the power unit and the cooling group. The whole of the body and underframe is constructed of mild steel, except for the driving cab which is a reinforced glass-fibre module carried on the forward portion of the underframe. The body is located on spigots in the bogie centre, and the weight is taken by four flexicoil springs on each bogie which carry a total weight of 22 tons.

The power bogies on the prototype were of the BT5 type, a strengthened version of the B4 bogie. The B4 was first used in 1956 and was based on an ORE design using coil suspension and long swing links with vertical, lateral and rotational damping by Koni dampers. The SKF roller-bearing axlebox is mounted in a radial arm and the monobloc 1,020mm (40in) wheels are shrunk onto a hollow axle and finished to a P8 profile. The total unsprung mass per axle came to 2,216kg (4,875lb) thus meeting the civil engineer's requirement.

In order to obtain the required braking power to allow 125mph operation within the existing signalling system it was necessary to use disc brakes, and the Girling disc pads are fitted on both sides of each wheel. In addition a cast-iron scrubber is used on the power car bogies to maintain tyre conditions for adhesion; this scrubber block is also used for the parking brake, which is operated by hydraulic pressure. On the prototypes the No 1 power car was fitted with the Westinghouse Westcode DW–1 pressure-controlled unit, while the No 2 car was equipped with Davies & Metcalf E70 electronically-controlled system. Both were operated by three train wires, which gave seven levels of braking. Both power cars have Davies & Metcalfe 2-stage 2A115 air compressors resiliently mounted underfloor. The braking throughout the train

The first revenue-earning service run of prototype HST unit No 252.001 took place on 5 May 1975. The unit is seen at Paddington, awaiting departure for Bristol and Weston-super-Mare. (*British Rail*)

is the standard 2-pipe system with electrical control to all bogies, each of which carries four disc brake cylinders.

The designed value for deceleration was 9 percent, which was obtained under both wet and dry conditions on test in June 1973; this gives a stopping distance from 125mph (200kph) of 1,765 metres against the 2,030 metres allowed for normal passenger trains from 100mph (160kph).

The driver's cab was produced by the BR Plastics Development Unit at Derby and consists of a 3-stage laminate of 2in (50mm) thickness with all conduits, air pipes and ventilation ducts incorporated in the walls. The central windscreen of 1in high-impact safety glass designed to withstand the impact of 2 lb (1kg) at 190mph (300kph) was fortuitously tested during trials by a piece of ballast which hit the screen at 130mph and just crazed the outer skin. The driver was placed centrally in the prototype, with a spare seat just behind and to one side, but this proved unsatisfactory and was changed in the production versions. Owing to the 12-month delay in starting the tests due to the driver problem, they had to be somewhat curtailed so as not to delay the introduction of the trains into commercial service.

During the initial high-speed testing which included runs at 143mph (230kph), first achieved on the 12 June 1973 between Thirsk and Tollerton, severe bogie hunting was encountered at 206kph and the lateral damper rates were increased. There were also problems with water getting into the traction motors. Because of the high noise level of the fans on these motors, the production models have separate blowers for cooling

purposes. There were also problems with the turbochargers and with a fractured engine oil sump. During heavy braking the smell from the disc brakes found its way into the passenger accommodation – this was overcome by closing the inlet ducts to the air-conditioning equipment when braking hard.

Other modifications decided on as a result of the testing programme were:

1. A modified turbocharger enabling the engine output to be increased to 2,500hp (1,865kW) to allow for an extra coach if necessary.
2. Since the train was to be run as a fixed-formation set, the auxiliaries and the train supply could be entirely ac at 415volts 50Hz, thus eliminating some motor alternator sets which had to be provided in each coach.
3. A modified load regulator for the main alternator was adopted based on a 3-phase thyristor bridge circuit in place of the original dc chopper circuit.
4. All auxiliary drives for the engines would be by 3-phase induction motors.
5. An increase in the luggage space obtained by moving the radiators nearer the engine. Space had been allowed for the fitting of a 16-cylinder engine, but this possibility was ruled out by considerations of weight.
6. A reshaped driver's cab allowing both crew members to sit alongside each other. It was found very important for the second man to look out for permanent way staff and to operate the warning horns, since every second counted in giving them time to get out of the way and 60yd could be covered in that time. The redesigned cab had a larger front window as well as side windows. The side buffers were replaced by a centre buffer and a folding coupler. Full air-conditioning was provided for the cab as well as better soundproofing. One weakness observed during a run in one of the cabs was that the windscreen leaked water, just as some of the locomotive screens do.

The production train design was due for May 1974 and the first of the 27 trains for the Western Region was planned for completion by September 1975. These

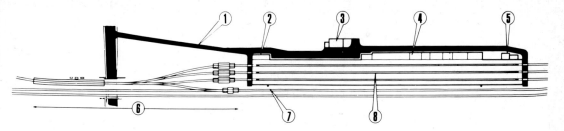

ST. PHILIPS MARSH   HIGH SPEED TRAIN DEPOT

1. ACCESS ROAD

2. WATER TANK and TOILETS

3. BOILER and COMPRESSOR HOUSE

4. STORES, MESS ROOM and SUPERVISORS OFFICE

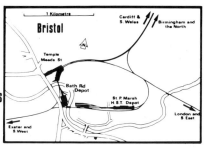

5. WATER SOFTENER and LUB OIL STORE

6. WASHING MACHINE

7. EXTERNAL FUELLING ROAD

8. SHED ROADS with CENTRE and SIDE PITS

Location and layout of St Philip's Marsh (Bristol) HST depot. (*British Rail*)

were to be followed by a further 42 sets by August 1977.

The prototype power cars were originally numbered 41.001/2 though strictly the Class 41 should have been allocated to the five original North British 2000hp diesel hydraulic locomotives Nos D600/4, but they were withdrawn before the current revised number scheme was instituted. The HST prototype was later numbered 252.001.

After further testing the prototype train entered public service on the 5 May 1975 working the 10.15 from Paddington to Weston-super-Mare. Before this the train had carried out around 120,000 miles of trial running. Operation continued throughout the summer of 1975 with two round trips each day, working at a maximum of 100mph to fit into the existing timetable.

On 4 October 1976 the 125mph services were started from Paddington to Bristol and to South Wales. The time to Bristol was reduced by 21 minutes and to Cardiff by 26 minutes, giving overall average speeds of 82mph. This service was initiated using the first eight trainsets.

By May 1977, with the 27 sets delivered, a full and faster timetable was introduced. The fastest train in the 1976 timetable was the 16.29 Reading to Bristol (Parkway) at 95.7mph (153kph): there were 11 trains at over 90mph and 48 at over 80mph, running a cumulative daily mileage of 3,647 miles.

To service these trains, two new depots were built specially, one at Old Oak Common (London) and one at St Philip's Marsh (Bristol). There were also refuelling points at Cardiff and at Swansea. The maintenance depots consist of three covered roads with centre and side pits, as well as a washing plant and a fuelling road. Bristol depot has through roads, but at

Old Oak it was necessary to have a dead end in three roads because of space limitations.

In 1976 Paxmans completed a new £1.5 million diesel engine test shop, principally for its Valenta engines. The six test cells could cater for a total output of 13,500kW at any one time. The total production for the previous year was quoted as 202,000kW, entailing a total testing time of over 9,000 hours. Some of the special UIC tests involved running times of up to 360 hours for any one engine.

1977 saw a complete Inter-City 125 timetable introduced for the Bristol and South Wales services, which required some runs to the working timetable at over 103mph. On the 7 May Jubilee Special runs were made between Bristol (Temple Meads) and Paddington (117.6 miles) in 68 minutes 23 seconds one way and 67 minutes 35 seconds the other at average speeds of 103.3mph (165kph) and 104.4mph (167kph) respectively. The unit was No 253.019 and the drivers were W. H. Francis and R. J. Sandcock for the up run and A. Williams and W. J. V. Jones for the down run. Just before this, in April, the Secretary of State for Transport had authorised a further 14 sets for the services to Plymouth and Penzance.

After nearly two years of intensive operation defects began to appear which had not shown up during the testing of the prototype set. Following the discovery of a fractured axlebox housing on a MkIII coach, a modified housing was designed and these were fitted in coach sets as soon as any one of the housings on that coach showed any signs of fracture. This exercise was almost complete when some engine defects showed up. They affected the cylinder heads, the turbochargers, the blade connecting rods and the sumps. The cylinder head trouble was due to poor foundry methods which were improved. The turbochargers suffered from fatigue cracks in the nozzle ring and brought a change in blade design with the material changed from

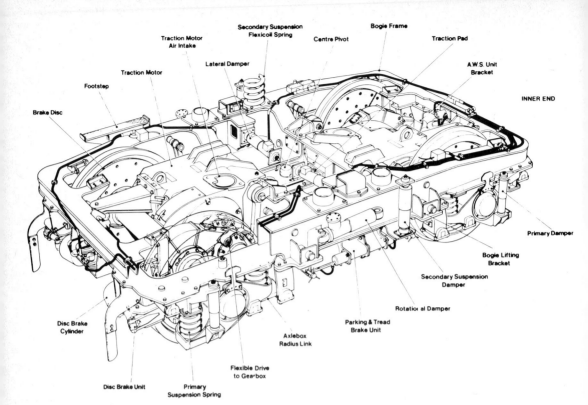

Drawing of HST power car bogie. (*British Rail*)

austenitic steel to Nimonic 75. The blade connecting rods suffered from fractures originating at the base of the bolt holes, and this was partly overcome by shortening the bolts and by chemically cleaning the threads, but there are still some problems reputedly connected with the tapped holes caused by nitriding. So far there is still debate as to whether bolt threads should be nitrided or not. Sump fractures were stated to be due to an inadequate weld in the sump rail, which has since been redesigned.

There were some electrical problems including the traction motor brushes, the alternator short-circuiting device and the main alternator exciter field contactor, but they have been modified to suit. There were also some fractures in the flexible drive links from the traction motors, but they now have a better standard of finish. When it is necessary to replace a link the complete set has to be replaced by a matched set in order to maintain dynamic balance.

There were and still are some troubles with the disc brakes both on the HST and on the MkIII locomotive-hauled coaches due to fractures near the fitted bolts which were at the corners of the discs. The fitted bolts have now been changed to the centre line of the pads and increased in size on the HST power cars from 13mm to 18mm, but this problem is not still fully cured.

In stopping an HST from 125mph in an emergency the energy to be dissipated is considerable and the heat dissipation rate on the discs is estimated at around 55 watts/sq cm. This compares with about 260 watts for a heavy commercial vehicle and about 350 watts for a jet aircraft. In the case of the HST the braking can be continuous for over one minute and can be applied several times in the course of a journey; in the case of the commercial vehicle the braking times are much shorter, but can be fairly frequent and in the case of an aircraft the braking times are well spaced out.

One further problem was the darkened patch above the driver's screen caused by the exhaust gas from the rear engine clinging to the trailing car body. This has almost been overcome by the fitting of a deflector plate 100mm above the power car roof, under which clean air is induced to form a boundary layer over the cab roof.

On the 8 May 1978 an HST125 service was inaugurated on the East Coast Main Line (ECML) between London (Kings Cross) and Aberdeen, the route of the Flying Scotsman, the Silver Jubilee and the Coronation expresses, for which the Gresley A4 Pacifics were built. The Flying Scotsman became an HST working from that date. It was also the route of one of the contenders in the 1895 Race to the North, when the 523-mile journey to Aberdeen was run in 520 minutes on this route. For long years after that the time taken to reach Edinburgh (393 miles) was $8\frac{1}{4}$ hours, and not until 1932 did that come down to $7\frac{1}{2}$ hours and then to six hours in 1937. Post-war running showed a deterioration until the coming of the Deltics (Class 55) when the times to Edinburgh were restored

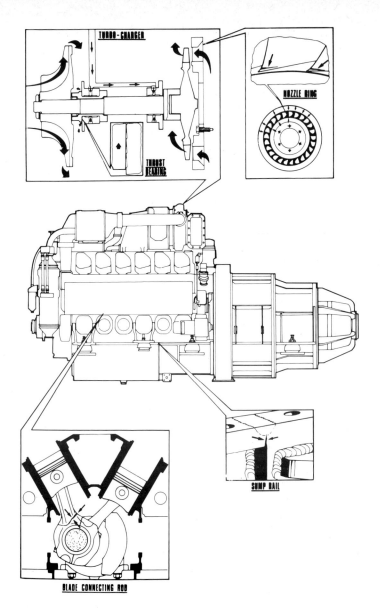

Valenta engine problems: fatigue cracks affecting the turbo charger, and the blade connecting rod, and fractures at the sump rail. (*D. Power*)

to six hours initially, then to 5½ hours after the first batch of permanent way improvements was completed in 1973. Before that several severe speed restrictions, particularly those at Peterborough (20mph), Newark (60mph), Selby (45mph), York (25mph) and Durham (30mph) had frustrated the 105mph capability of the Deltics. A further series of track improvements was taking place when the HST service was inaugurated, and these works imposed temporary speed limits in places as, for example, Tallington and at Claypole to 20mph, at Newark to 30mph, with 20mph restrictions at Teesdale, Low Fell, Morpeth, Alnmouth and Beal. By May 1982 the route was cleared for 125mph most of the way to Newcastle, with restrictions below

100mph only at Selby (60mph), York (35mph) and at Durham (75mph). The Selby limit was overcome in 1983 with the opening of the Selby diversion line in which a new 125mph railway was built avoiding Selby coalfield and removing Selby from the through East Coast route. Most trains stopped at York and Durham anyway. Present timing are 188 minutes to Newcastle (268½ miles) with a best time of 177 minutes (91mph). The average time to Edinburgh is 285 minutes for the 393 miles, with the fastest run in 275 minutes (85.7mph). To Aberdeen (523 miles) the best time is 437 minutes (71.8mph). At last the 1895 time was bettered, and not just by one light racing train.

The 32 sets for the ECML contained an extra second-class car, making it a 2+8 formation. For a few months after September 1980 a further coach was added, making a 2+9 formation, but this upset the

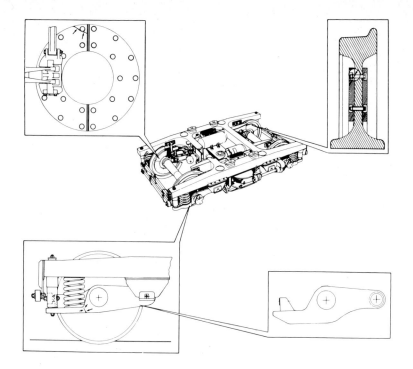

Fractures of the braking discs near the bolts at the corners; fractures of the axlebox housing casting near the spring bed on the HST Mk III coaches. (*D. Power*)

9-car Class 254 IC125 unit on the Eastern Region. (*Brian Webb*)

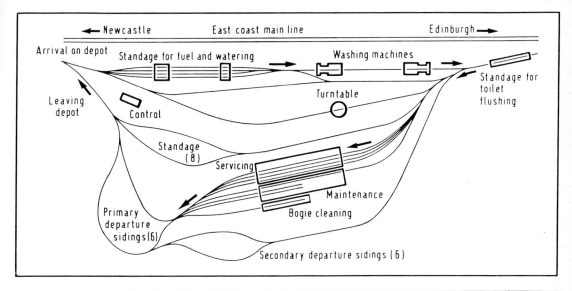

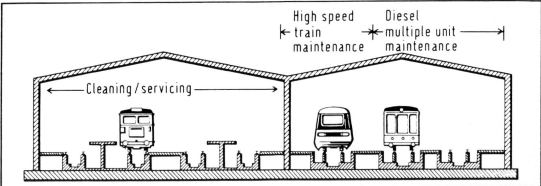

Layout and cross-section of Heaton HST depot, Eastern Region

timekeeping and the arrangements at the servicing depots so it did not last long.

These sets were mostly allocated to Neville Hill Depot at Leeds (17 sets) with five sets each at Craigentinny (Edinburgh), Heaton (Newcastle), and Bounds Green (London). The operating diagrams required the use of 25 sets with overnight stabling at Craigentinny (6) Heaton (4), Neville Hill (7) and Bounds Green (8) thus calling for an availability of 78 percent. It had been intended to uprate the engines to 2,500hp for this service in order to cope with the extra coach, but the turbocharger problems precluded this step. With the original output of 4,500hp for the whole train this made timekeeping rather uncertain on this route, particularly when there were extra track repairs in force.

The examinations carried out at the various service depots consist of an A Examination carried out every two days, with checks on brakes and with samples of engine oil taken for analysis. The B, C & D examinations are carried out at one, 3- and 6-monthly intervals for more detailed checks and for filter changes. Every year the whole train is returned to BREL main workshops after 200/250,000 miles for tyre turning and component replacements. If tyre turning is required at the 6-monthly interval this is carried out on the ground lathe at Doncaster.

Inspection periods for traction motor gearboxes and in particular the gearbox oil levels were called into question after an Inter-City 125 unit was derailed at Northallerton in 1979 at 70mph after the gearbox of the leading axle of the front bogie seized, probably locking solid as the train left York. A false flange was worn on the wheel tread which derailed the wheels when passing through points at Northallerton, damaging the track and leading to the derailment of the entire train, fortunately without major casualties. There were also faults in the wheel slide protection indications so that the locked axle was not detected by the driver. Heaton depot is also equipped with a 20-tonne crane, by which power units can be exchanged in emergency without having to send the whole train or even the power car to the main BREL works.

While the Eastern and Scottish Regions were getting used to their new HST sets the Western Region decided to attempt a world record run and on 10 April 1979 when the only permanent speed restrictions were the

80mph at Reading and 100mph at Swindon. The 09.20 ran from Paddington to Chippenham (94 miles) in $50\frac{1}{2}$ minutes, an average of 111.6mph; this was 5mph faster than the record claimed by the Japanese Railways on its Shinkansen electric service.

This was followed in August 1979 by the introduction of HST sets on the West of England line to Plymouth and to Penzance, which included the Cornish Riviera express (originating from 1904), but its former fans would hardly have recognised it with all the stops it made on its journey. In the days of steam the original 10.30 Limited stopped only three times after Plymouth and took 389 minutes for the 305 miles to Penzance. The HST version stopped first at Reading and then eight more times before arriving at Penzance, but it did it in exactly 305 minutes. This hardly seems to be the best utilisation for this sort of train, with a general speed limit of 90mph after Reading and with even 70mph rarely obtainable between Plymouth and Penzance. This service would seem best suited to the use of a different gear ratio, and this coupled with a reduced engine output could ensure a longer component life.

The next versions of the HST were put into service on the so-called Heart Line, running between the South West and the North East. These services started in September 1981, with the full service timetable in May 1982. The formation was different with only one first class car but five seconds. A batch of HSTs for the former Midland line from St Pancras to Sheffield and Derby was acquired largely by reallocating sets from the WR and rediagramming remaining WR sets to cover a greater daily mileage. An HST unit had been tried out on the Midland line in April 1978 and had run the 128 miles from Derby to London in 135 minutes, but this is now timed at 101 minutes. Some have been making stops at Bedford (originally unintended) in order to supplement the ailing Class 127 DMUs which were scheduled for withdrawal when the Bedford electrification scheme came into force. Electric services

were due to have started in 1982, but had to be postponed due to problems over manning and eventually got under way in 1983.

There are still a few operational problems to be solved, principally in connection with the engine and with the brakes. It is natural that the application and removal of so much energy in such a short time should present difficulties, but these will no doubt be overcome. The engine problems are mostly due to water leaking into the oil, which necessitates sampling every two days. It is hoped that the use of a cast-iron crankcase will help by making a more rigid block, and over a third of the engines have had these fitted. One final piece of advice by a BR engineer was to take a screwdriver with you when travelling by HST, since the toilet door locks are prone to jam and it might be the only way of getting out! On a matter of detail, at the end of 1983 new style APT pattern livery with dark blue at window level flanked by light grey above and below and a red band just below the windows was applied the two sets on the WR for use on 'executive' services. Some coaches have APT style seats.

Apart from the electrification schemes the HST125 as a concept can be said to be the most successful of the British Railways modernisation plans, and is amply justified by the results being obtained. Acknowledgement of the success of the HST125 has come from Australia where eight train sets in 6- or 7-coach formation have been built by the Commonwealth Engineering (NSW) Pty Ltd of Granville for the New South Wales Railway system. These are running on five routes out of Sydney for journeys of up to 320 miles, with considerable savings in overall times. Already they have set up an Australian speed record of 114mph. For these trains, known in Australia as the Inter-City XPT, seventeen sets of equipment have been supplied by the Brush Electrical Engineering Company and by Paxman Diesels; it is anticipated that up to 13 complete trains will be built, each with two power cars as on the BR IC125 sets.

8 APT — railcar to electric train

APT is the official designation of the Advanced Passenger Train, but it could equally be applied to 'Assorted Prototype Trains'. It can be questioned whether the APT should be included in a treatise on railcars since in its latest form it is an electric unit for operation on the West Coast Main Line 25kV route, but it was not originally designed in that form and it certainly first ran as a self-propelled unit.

In origin it goes further back than the HST, and it could be said to have started when the new BR Research Laboratories were opened at Derby in May 1964. In themselves these could also be traced back to the embryo research department started by the London Midland & Scottish Railway in 1933, which was initiated strictly as a service to the major operating and engineering departments, but from that humble beginning it grew to its present dominance of the Derby scene.

One of the functions of the new laboratory was the study of the behaviour of steel wheels on steel rails, in order to improve riding qualities and stability, which needs arose from operating speeds. Initially this study was concerned with freight vehicles, since they were the principal drag on the improvement of overall operating speeds. When the new designs of 2-axle freight vehicles were proved capable of working at up to 140mph, attention was turned to passenger vehicles in order to ascertain the safe maximum operating speeds without having to build completely new tracks — that was the option chosen by Japan for the New Tokaido and later by the SNCF for the Paris–Lyon lines.

Apart from Brunel's line from London to Bristol, the railways of the UK were not laid out for high-speed travel. When the LMS carried out its high-speed non-stop run from Euston to Glasgow in November 1936, during which the 401 miles were run in 352 minutes, there were no fewer than 43 speed restrictions (equivalent to one every nine miles) with some as low as 20mph. Even as recently as 1977 a footplate run on a Class 87 electric locomotive revealed 22 speed restrictions on the 100mph line between Crewe and Carlisle (a mere 143 miles) most being due to curves with radii less than 56 chains (1128 metres).

The conventional railway wheel is turned to a conical taper to give a differential effect on curves, but this can also have the effect of producing hunting (a side-to-side movement) on straight track. On the LNER Silver Jubilee the wheels on the last bogie had to have parallel tyres to eliminate severe hunting. One of the results of the research department's investigations into wheel/rail reaction showed that if the rigidly restricted axlebox were to be given some freedom of fore-and-aft movement this, combined with increased wheel cone angle, could produce a measure of self-guidance without any increase in the flange loading of the wheels.

That in turn led to a further problem in the design of the suspension, in that soft suspension is desirable for good steering and hard suspension for good·stability; the combination of these findings has been the fundamental object of the APT suspension design.

This research having shown that up to 155mph (250kph) was a feasible operating speed, it was clear that such a speed could only be used on existing track if some form of carriage tilt could be adopted, to increase the speed round curves and thus eliminate the number of speed restrictions which would nullify a high top speed on the straight track. These investigations showed that a tilt angle of 9 degrees would be needed in order to limit the discomfort to passengers when rounding curves at the speeds envisaged.

Proposed APT timings on some principal Inter City journeys from London were computed as:

Desination	Time (minutes)	Saving (minutes)
Bristol	67	33
Cardiff	86	41
Leeds	105	51
Manchester	120	31
Newcastle	140	75
Edinburgh	220	125

In March 1967 the concept of the APT was revealed by the Labour Minister of Transport (Mrs Barbara Castle) while in the following year the Government agreed to share in the costs of development, then estimated as £9.8 million.

APT-POP space frame units, designed to test bogies and tilt mechanism for the Advanced Passenger Train. (*British Rail*)

The original concept was based on the use of one Rolls-Royce Dart gas turbine rated at 1,500hp to each vehicle and driving on one bogie with a separate gas turbine driven auxiliary set for each coach. By 1969 the design was amended to that of separate power cars and construction of the first experimental train (APT-E) was authorised.

This design comprised a 4-car set having two power cars, each driven by four Leyland 350 automotive gas turbines, each set to deliver 300hp, with a fifth similar engine for auxiliary power supplies.

To achieve the desired aim of 16hp/ton the total train weight was stipulated not to exceed 150 tonnes. This actually worked out at 145 tonnes, made up of 49 tonnes for each power car and 23.5 tonnes for each trailer, with individual axle loadings of just over 17 tonnes per axle.

Each power car was carried on a power bogie in which were mounted two AEI253AY nose-suspended electric traction motors. This arrangement was only adopted for the APT-E power bogies since the high unsprung weight with a nose suspended motor would not have been acceptable for normal commercial use at the speeds intended. The gear ratio allowed a safe top speed of 197mph (315kph). The motors were self-ventilated with a drip-proof cover. The bogie had an air-sprung transom on which the tilt jacks were mounted, and the wheel sets were located in yokes with

a twin-coil spring primary suspension with hydraulic dampers.

The driving wheel diameter was 36in (914mm) and the braking on these bogies was by rheostatic dynamic system from 155mph down to 45mph, below which tread shoes on normal brake hangers worked on the wheel tread. The traction motor fields were excited from the main alternators and the energy generated was dissipated through a fan-cooled resistor stack in the car body.

The inner end of the power car was suspended on one end of an intermediate articulated bogie and it was these bogies that embraced most of the novel features of the APT design. These bogies consisted of a longtitudinal beam on which the body pivots were located well outside the wheel base with an overhang of 1.73m (44in). The beam itself was supported on an intermediate frame between the two wheelsets which were quite independent of each other. The wheelsets were in separate yokes similar to a pony truck which could be steered by the wheel/rail reaction and which were coupled to the intermediate frame and to the longtitudinal beam by springs and dampers. The suspension between the beam and the intermediate frame was soft to give a comfortable ride, but the rest of the system was hard and self-levelling in order to promote a non-tilting platform to which the tilting jacks could be fitted. The power bogies on this train set carried a nomenclature E1 numeral while the articulated trailer bogies were designated by E1T.

The wheel sets on the trailer bogies consisted of 750mm (30in) diameter wheels mounted on hollow

The experimental APT-E, driven by four 350hp gas turbines, at Swindon on 10 August 1975, having attained 152mph on a test run. (*British Rail*)

axles which contained a hydrokinetic brake capable of a retardation rate of 1.5m/sec/sec (2.2mph/sec) from a top speed of 250kph (155mph). This system of braking was judged necessary in order to enable speeds of up to 250kph to be run without having to resignal the existing lines, which were laid out for a stopping distance of 2,040 metres (2,230 yards or 1.27 miles). These braking rates could not be achieved using tread or disc brakes and the hydrokinetic system was adopted as being the only possible solution.

This braking system consists of a fluid coupling similar to those used on the engine output side of the DMU railcar sets which could be filled with a water-glycol mixture and where the heat generated could be cooled in a radiator system. The energy dissipation could be up to 35MJ per axle with a heat rate of 1.43MW (equivalent to seven hundred 2kW electric heaters). This system was only effective down to 80kph (50mph) below which a hydraulically-operated clasp brake was automatically brought into action. This whole braking system was to prove the principal problem during the trial running on the West Coast Main Line in 1982.

The power cars for the APT–E which were built by the Metro-Cammel Company were 23m (75.4ft) long,

2.685m (8.8ft) wide and 3.64m (11.94ft) high; they were of steel construction, with a nose cone built by BREL. The contained four Leyland 350 2-shaft automotive gas turbines set to deliver 298hp at 27°C ambient, with the output shaft geared to a Houchin 400V alternator running at 3,000rpm. Each pair of alternators fed one of the dc traction motors through silicon rectifiers. A fifth similar turbine drove an auxiliary alternator running at 1,500rpm and supplying power at 415volts 3-phase 50Hz with an output of 150kVA. Either of these auxiliaries could supply sufficient power for the whole 4-car unit.

The combustion air was taken through automotive type air filters mounted in the bodysides, and the exhaust was through silencers to a roof-mounted cowl. The turbines ran on class A diesel fuel fed from a ring main supplied from the underfloor tank through an air separator under pressure. There was automatic or manned fire protection by a BCF gas spray system with temperature detectors. A Worthington-Simpson MTV36 air compressor supplied air at 962kN sq m (140lb/sq in) for air springs, turbine nozzle controls, horns and brakes. The driver's cab in the nose cone had a single central seat behind a high-impact Triplex safety-glass screen 19mm (0.75in) thick. The control console had a brake handle on one side, and the power handle on the other side which set all eight traction alternator field currents. The paralleling of all eight outputs was to give some problems during the early test runs. The instrument panel in front of the driver held a central speedometer (in kph) with an accelerometer (G percent) on the left and an ammeter for traction motor current on the other side. The train speed was measured by a Doppler radar unit mounted under the nose cone, which bounced the signal back from the track and was thus unaffected by wheel slip or change in wheel diameter. Wheel slip and wheel slide protection was provided by separate axle-generated speed signals.

The two trailer car bodies were of double-skin aluminium semi-monocoque construction with double-glazed windows and were built by the Aircraft Division of GEC Traction at Accrington. The solebars and cross beams at the suspension point were the only items of steel construction, while the floor was an aluminium alloy sandwich with a balsa wood core.

The saloon was 17.2m (56.4ft) long by 2.58m (8.46ft) wide by 2.03m (6.66ft) high and for test purposes these cars were filled with instrumentation equipment. The trailer car bodies weighed only four tons and had no passenger doors as these were provided in a special spherical pivot between adjacent vehicle bodies and mounted over the articulated bogies. The whole 4-car set was 87.62 metres (287.5ft) long and would have seated at a maximum only 128 passengers.

The APT–E was completed by May 1972, but while it was being finished and undergoing strain gauging and other laboratory tests a couple of space frame vehicles called APT–POP had been built for the preliminary testing of bogies and suspension systems. The bogies on the POP cars were not quite the same as the APT–E bogies and were designated H4X for the end bogies and H3X for the articulated ones. These units were locomotive-hauled and had commenced trials in September 1971 on the line between Melton Junction and Edwalton (Notts), a disused length of track formerly linking Melton Mowbray with Nottingham, which was specially refurbished for the APT trials and became known as the Old Dalby test track.

In addition to the APT–POP trials a former Hastings line buffet car with straight sides built to the restricted width of 8ft 2in was fitted with prototype APT end trailer bogies and tested on conventional track at up to 6 degree tilt. Both this coach and the POP cars carried out trials on main lines, hauled by Class 47 diesel locomotives at up to 100mph and by Class 86 and Class 87 electric locomotives at up to 125mph. Finally, in order to check the predicted overturning cant deficiency of 25 degrees a scrap MkII coach modified to represent APT mass distribution was loose shunted at increasing speeds until it overturned round a disused leg of a triangle between Deal Junction and Kearnsey Loop Junction near Dover with a radius of 9 chains. Overturning occurred at 24.3 degrees.

The APT–E commenced its proving trials between Derby and Duffield on 25 July 1972 and then ran into trouble with the drivers' union (ASLEF) which as in the case of the HST held up development testing for over a year; driver training did not commence fully

until August 1973. Meantime, plans were ahead to produce two further versions, one with gas turbine and one with electric propulsion, but in 1974 Leyland Motors dropped out of the gas turbine market and all the design effort was transferred to the electric prototype APT–P. The requirement of the West Coast Main Line with its then limitation of 100mph took precedence over the Eastern and the Western lines which could use the 125mph HST diesel trains.

Development testing of the APT–E then got under way in October 1974 with operation on the Old Dalby track but that was limited to 125mph, and not until August 1975 when running between Reading and Swindon allowed higher speeds was the top speed of 151mph (242kph) eventually achieved. In October 1975 trial runs were made between St Pancras and Leicester in which the 99 miles were run in 58 minutes at 102mph.

This route of the former Midland Railway had never been built as a main line throughout. Speed restrictions for curves particularly at St Albans, Luton, Bedford, Wellingborough, Market Harborough and Wigston showed that the APT could save 22min on the journey time over conventional diesel-hauled trains at that time. Now with IC125 operation on this line the time to Leicester has been reduced to 72min and with the hope of the electrification being extended from Bedford it is possible that the APT might operate on this line in the future.

During its testing period on the Western Region, slipstream measurements were undertaken on station platforms and on passing trains. The value of the nose shape developed in tests at the British Aerospace tunnel at Brough and on a model test track at Pendine showed how well-designed trains could pass each other at high speed with the minimum of interference. These tests also showed the value of a smooth external finish and the absence of breaks in the external contour of the train formation. These features also help to reduce the risk of overturning these very light coaches in exposed windy situations, and reduce the effects on overhead electrical equipment and the pantographs of passing trains. Considerable testing was also undertaken in the measurement of adhesion factors to help in the understanding of braking limitations at high speeds. Following the tests the APT–E train was withdrawn after completing less than 4,000 miles and was sent to the National Railway Museum at York, where it now rests.

While the APT–E had been carrying out its testing programme for bogies, braking systems and tilt mechanism the design of the first production prototype sets (APT–P) had been commenced in 1973 and the construction of three trains was authorised in 1974.

Since the main commercial demand was for a speed improvement on the difficult West Coast line which was due to be electrified through to Glasgow by the time the APT was due to come into service this next APT application was designed to use electric

Detail of Type BT12 leading bogie on APT-P driving trailer. (*British Rail*)

propulsion and was originally envisaged in three different formations:

A 1 power car and 11 trailers.
Speed 135mph (215kph)
B 2 power cars and 12 trailers.
Speed 170mph (270kph)
C 2 power cars and 14 trailers.
Speed 160mph (255kph)

In these the power cars would be in the centre of the train and each would be of 3MW comprising four 750kW traction motors driving through right-angled gears. The motors which were to be fully springborne were mounted in the car body, which would be a steel monocoque structure with a body weight of only 11.8 tons. The drive from the motors was through a transfer gearbox to which the hydrokinetic brake would be coupled, and then through a cardan shaft to the final drive gearbox on each of the four driving axles.

The end vehicle in each train was a driving trailer with a special bogie (BT12) at the driving end and with the other end resting on the intermediate trailer bogie (type BT11) used throughout the rest of the train in its articulated arrangement. The mid-train power cars effectively split the train in two from the passengers' viewpoint, which would have meant duplicate refreshment facilities as it would have been undesirable for passengers to pass through in normal service.

The power bogie (BP17A) was different from that used on the APT–E both in drive and in suspension; it also included a special linkage for the pantograph

platform to obviate the problem of tilting on curves.

The passenger-carrying trailer cars were constructed in aluminium using wide section extrusions for the full vehicle length. In the APT–E a spherical pivot plug was used between the cars in which the doors were mounted, but this was found to be unsatisfactory, and the cars in the APT–P had the doors incorporated in the bodysides with one door in each side at diagonally opposite corners. With this arrangement the passenger accommodation was arranged for 72 second-class seats or 47 first-class seats within a vehicle length of 21 metres (69ft), and by the use of lightweight seats and chemical toilets the body weight was kept down to 4.7 tons.

The air-conditioning, tilt control and brake control units are arranged as replaceable modules in easily removable packs under the coach floor. The air-conditioning system was designed to recirculate 80 percent of the air through carbon filters and the intake and exhaust areas for the other 20 percent were sealed on entry into tunnels to protect the passengers from pressure surges.

The driver's cab was redesigned as on the HST to allow a second man to sit alongside the driver as a lookout since the time allowance for warning permanent way staff would be even less than for the HST, and split-second operation of the warning horn could be crucial to their survival, although other forms of warning initiated at the working site by track circuit operation from the approaching train are also under investigation.

The construction of these prototype APT-P train sets began in 1976 by which time the French Experimental 5-car gas-turbine *Train à Grand Vitesse* (TGV.001) had run 306,000km; of this 1,418km had been run at over 300kph (187mph). In December 1975 a speed of 318kph (199mph) had been attained, but this was still below the 205mph achieved by French electric locomotives in March 1955. The production electric TGV for the new SNCF line between Paris and Lyons was to comprise eight trailer coaches between two power cars each of 3,150kW making a train weight of 410 tonnes (15.4kW/tonne). The comparable APT would have been the 2+12 formation with 6,000kW for a weight of 463 tonnes, or 12.9kW/tonne. The APT was intended to provide 592 seats against 384 for the TGV. During the building of the first APT vehicles considerable testing was being carried out on the pantograph system as well as on brakes, transmission, air-conditioning equipment, doors and toilets.

The power cars for the APT-P consisted of a steel monocoque shell mounted on two 4-wheel bogies, with a central walkway through for emergency, and with no control facilities of its own. The bogies were of a new design type BP17A and the wheelsets which carried the right-angled final drive weighed only 1.5 tonnes unsprung; they were carried in yokes with primary coil suspension to the bogie frame. The coach body was carried by four flexicoils to each bogie actuated by the tilt mechanism. The pantograph was carried by a separate system of self-levelling stays unaffected by the tilting operation. The one pantograph, which had

Type BT11 APT-P intermediate trailing bogie. (*British Rail*)

three stage suspension, collected the 25kV alternating current and fed a busbar mounted on the coach roof which could couple up to the next power car to avoid the use of two pantographs so near to each other. The current then fed through transformers and thyristors to the four 750kW ASEA traction motors mounted in the car body. The total power car weight was 69 tonnes, thus allowing 57 tonnes for the 3MW of power equipment. The train auxiliary load of 400kW was supplied from a motor-alternator set carried in the trailer next to the power car and this load (200kW for each half train) could be supplied in emergency by a 200kW diesel alternator set in the driving trailer just behind the driver's cab.

The first power car, No SC49003, was completed by December 1978 and it was subjected to tests using the two prototypes HST Class 252 power cars as control units. These were fitted with special driving consoles to enable the APT power car to be either diesel-hauled or to work on the electrified line. By March 1979 the second power car had been through its tests and the first prototype train was assembled as a 2+6 formation with the two power cars between two 3-car trailer sets.

Subject to delays due to industrial disputes, testing took place to prove the braking, tilt operation, track forces and pantograph performance; during these tests a maximum speed of 162mph (260kph) was achieved

No longer a self-contained railcar train, one of the electric APT-P 2+12 formations on test, photographed at Beattock in December 1981 (*British Rail*)

on 20 December 1979 at Quintinshill, the site in 1915 of the worst disaster in British railway history. During 1979 the second prototype train was commissioned and used primarily for driver training; the third train, consisting of a 2+8 formation commenced endurance running between Glasgow and London (Euston).

The driving technique for the APT calls for a different approach to the usual speed limits imposed for conventional trains, since they do not apply to the APT. In order to reduce braking and subsequent accelerations to a minimum the driver's cab is provided with a continuous display which shows the maximum permissible speed at any time. This also gives warning of normal or special speed restrictions that can be expected in the next section of track. This is achieved by the use of over 2,000 Plessey transponders mounted on the sleepers and actuated by signals transmitted from an aerial mounted underneath the train. The signal frequency is 147kHz and is strong enough to actuate the response without any power supply to the rail-mounted unit. The coded message of 80 data bits can be sent at speeds even above the designed top speed of 250kph. Fail-safe operation is provided, which can apply the brakes in an emergency.

By late 1981 the three trains had run for over 137,000 miles and in the course of testing certain problems came to light, primarily affecting the most novel features – indeed the primary equipment on which the whole APT concept was founded – such as the tilt control and the braking systems.

In the APT-P the sensing accelerometer was mounted on the bogie bolster, but this did not give a rapid enough response. In a MkII system there were two additional sensing circuits to separate the curve-induced signals from those sensed due to track irregularities, but this was still not satisfactory and in a MkIII system the accelerometer was moved to the bogie frame with a filter to remove the track effects, and this proved satisfactory. This was further improved by mounting the accelerometer for each car on the bogie of the preceding vehicle. One further problem was that of oil cleanliness due to the fine apertures used in the feeds to the tilt cylinders. This was rectified by the use of a special portable oil cleaning machine in the workshops and in the maintenance depots, backed up by a one micron filter on each bogie.

Fears existed that incorrect hard-over tilt in the wrong direction could cause passing trains to hit each other, and to overcome this a detection unit sensed incorrect tilt, returned the vehicle to the upright position and locked it in that state.

There were problems with the transmission gearboxes primarily due to loss of oil from the labyrinth seals. This was largely due to high oil temperatures and was caused primarily by the blockage of the oil jets by debris; it was overcome by better protection and the fitting of additional oil coolers. This overheating also resulted in oil leakages due to deterioration in the seals. The oil got onto the wheel rims and affected the adhesion factor; sometimes this was as low as 7 percent. It was at times difficult to maintain performance even on level track and considerable wheelslip was experienced on the climbs to Shap and Beattock summits. The Bo-Bo electric locomotives with their 20-ton axle loading have difficulties on these sections under conditions of moist rail, particularly in the Lune gorge, but in spite of sophisticated methods of wheelslip control a good driver can anticipate and overcome such problems. It was also found that the best wheelslip protection is given by the inherent torque/speed characteristics of the series traction motor.

The intermediate reduction gearbox was necessary because the offset position of the traction motors resulted from the need to provide an emergency side-corridor through the power cars in the centre of the train. This was due to the theory that only one pantograph should be used because of the bouncing effect caused by one pantograph reacting on another through the overhead centenary. It was not considered possible to run an 25kV busline the length of the train as on the French TGV because of the varying tilt angles of adjacent coaches, but with two power cars together in the train centre they have a 25kV overhead jumper system since the adjoining pantograph platforms would not tilt.

The intermediate gearboxes also provided a suitable location for the hydrokinetic brake on the power cars and this type gave almost no trouble in service. Rheostatic braking had been considered as on the APT–E, but that would have entailed larger and more costly traction motors and would only have applied around 25 percent of the braking effort. It would also have meant extra control gear and would not have had the same fail-safe features. The major problem was with the hydrokinetic brakes on the trailer bogie axles, but before considering these other problems emerged during the trials and testing of the three prototype trains.

One was passenger reaction regarding train motion arising from the tilt, which varied with the prejudice of the observer. Some complained of actual sickness, but this was usually found to be of the 'morning' sort as most of the cases were on the first train out of Glasgow. There were no reported cases after dark so it was assumed that the effect of unexpected horizon movement was to blame. Standing or walking passengers were also more affected than seated ones since the reaction when standing was greater than with the transition in a normal train, due to the speed of application of the tilt. This particularly affected the dining car staff who would be more likely to be facing a window. There were also effects at the highest operational speed of long wavelength track irregularities, and these were worse on the West Coast Main Line with locomotive operation than on many others where the IC125 trains were at work – a travesty for the once so-called 'Premier Line'.

Two other problems came to light during the tests. One was that the coach lighting had been arranged so that 25 percent was battery-fed and the rest supplied by motor-alternator sets, with the result that on neutral gaps 75 percent of the lights went out or dimmed. In future designs the lighting is to be 100 percent battery-fed. The other problem arose with icing of the train air supplies at below −15 deg C, which showed up in the cold spell in December 1981. The moisture extraction was inadequate and extra driers were installed. There were also instances of ice build-up on the pantographs during that cold spell.

The real major problem was with the hydrokinetic brakes on the trailer car bogies which were built into the hollow axles. The actuating toroid in the axle casing was made of aluminium, to keep the unsprung weight within the stipulated limits, and this suffered from three sorts of troubles. First there were fluid leakages from the large diameter hoses and from the carbon face seal within the brake unit. The next problem was blade disintegration due to loosening of the dowel pins in the fluid seal units, but the third trouble was with the toroid connections to the outer axle casing. Due the high operating temperature the toroid material elongated with a thinning at the axle joint which caused the bolts to work loose. On one occasion in 1980 an axle parted in the third car, causing a derailment at 200kph, fortunately without harm. During this incident not only was a reverse curve successfully negotiated, but it was not noticed by the driver and power was not shut off until twenty seconds after it happened. This was a testimony to the strength of the couplings, since the derailed car was in front of the power cars. As a result of this it was considered too dangerous to rely on this system of braking and the low-speed clasp brakes also sometimes failed to release thus causing overheating of the wheels and once the movement of a wheel on its axle. Any brake assembly hinged at the bottom seems inherently wrong since it does not naturally release of its own weight as on a top-hung arrangement; moreover the wheel tread brakes being of composition material also did nothing to improve adhesion as a cast iron block does.

Indeed many of the APT's problems seem to have arisen from the philosophy of the whole concept in exploring uncharted waters and getting away from traditional railway thinking. While that in itself is no bad thing, inevitably in putting all these new ideas in one package there would be problems but it was probably unwise to have ignored past and proved experience in some of the detail. By contrast the success of the Inter-City 125 HST has undoubtedly stemmed from its conventional use of features proved in service over a number of years.

In order to achieve a train reliability of 20,000km per casualty, which was considered the very minimum desirable, this was found to entail at least one million individual vehicle-kilometres per casualty, and this was nowhere like being obtained even with such items as the tilt system being designed with almost complete duplication. There were just too many novel features in one design. Even in the search for lightness some of the components in the passenger accommodation were found to be too flimsy for everyday use.

As a result of the decision to drop the hydrokinetic brake the only other high-speed braking system currently available is the disc brake system as used on the HST125 and the next generation of APT is designed to use this system. Since the heat dissipation of the disc brake is considerably less per axle than for the hydrokinetic type more axles are necessary, and the articulation arrangement is to be dropped in favour of conventional bogies. Apart from the fact that the tilting arrangement is still being retained, this brings the design concept round to what most practical railway engineers consider that it should be, namely an electric HST although even this proposal seemed to be a doubtful proposition early in 1984 with thinking turning towards locomotive haulage for 125mph trains. The re-designed version was to have been known as the APT–U, but because of unfavourable press coverage the APT brand name is to be finally exorcised and following the HST style the new concept will be known as Inter-City 225 or whatever the metric introductory speed is likely to be.

Before the current design there was one final layout of the original concept known as the APT–S. This was a 1+10 formation with a power car at one end and a driving trailer at the other. This would have given an output of 3,000kW for a train weight of 370 tons and would have been adequate for the intended speed of 125mph with power in hand to raise this speed at a later date if found practicable. The arrangement with the power cars in the centre of the train had some disadvantages and it was said that it might be dangerous for passengers to have to pass through the corridor of a power car, particularly those with heart pacemakers.

The latest proposals will make for easier handling of the vehicles in workshops, and the bogies proposed will be a disc braked version of the former APT end trailer bogie type BT12. In the new power cars the driver's cab will occupy the space previously taken up by one of the motors, reducing the output to 2,250kW. The power car will thus have two different bogies, the leading on designated A1P with one motor, the other a type BP17 with two motors. The power car weight is proposed as 67.9 tonnes, with a maximum axle load of 17.4 tonnes. The trailer cars, of which there will be 10 or 12, will use a BT30 bogie with a tilt mechanism, but even this may be abandoned if acceptable timings can be worked without this feature. The seating proposed in the IC225 is for 499 in the 2+10 formation and 643 in the 2+12 arrangement, with overall weights of 505 tonnes and 579 tonnes respectively. The power per tonne in the latter version will thus amount to 10.4hp.

When the original APT was conceived by Dr Sidney Jones, the railway system was in the course of emerging from the steam era into the early years of modernisation, and as a result of the efforts of his team to improve train riding enormous benefits have resulted, particularly in the HST trains. The application of aircraft technology to the environment of the steel rail has not been quite so fortunate, but the expenditure to date (said to be around £37 million) is quite modest at under 70p per head of population. Several other countries have tried out a tilt system of operation in an endeavour to improve speeds on existing track, but most have not persisted; if BR can successfully retain this feature for the higher speeds it may well have been worthwhile.

Type	Propulsion	Power (hp)	Weight (tonnes)	Seats	Speed mph	HP per tonne
APT–POP	Locomotive	–	–	–	125	–
APT–E	Gas Turbine	2,400	145	128	155	16.5
APT–P(1+11)	Electric	4,000	410	520	133	9.8
APT–P(2+12)	Electric	8,000	507	592	169	15.8
APT–P(2+14)	Electric	8,000	563	736	158	14.2
APT–S(1+10)	Electric	4,000	370	503	125	10.8
APT–U(2+10)	Electric	6,000	505	499	125	11.9
APT–U(2+12)	Electric	6,000	579	643	125	10.4

9 Railbuses

To complete the railcar story this final chapter looks at railbuses. During World War I thousands of troops were forced to ride in European 4-wheel box cars labelled *Hommes Quarante. Chevaux Huite*, and though the seating was more pleasant in the 4-wheel railbus vehicles on British Rail than in those French vans, the ride according to some was not a lot better. Most railbuses also seated just over the regulation 40, the greatest number being 56 seats.

Apart from early four-wheel railcars of the turn of the century, the first of the vehicles in this category, though not strictly labelled railbus, were some 4-wheel units built by the British United Traction Company in 1952. There were seven powered cars, each driven by one AEC 125hp diesel engine with the fluid flywheel and Wilson 4-speed gearbox driving onto one axle: each weighed 15 tons, seating 34 in the motor seconds and 28 in the motor brake seconds. There were also four trailer cars weighing 10.5 tons, and each seating 48 passengers.

These sets were made up into three car units comprising one of each type of power car with one trailer in between. The whole set thus weighed 40.5 tons and seated 110 passengers, all second class.

The first of these units was demonstrated near Gerrards Cross on 23 May 1952 and later went into service between Wellingborough and Higham Ferrers. The other two sets started life on the line between Watford Junction and St Albans, where their predecessors were known as the 'Bricket Wood Flyer'; that was when the branch train sometimes consisted of a standard BR 2–6–4T hauling two coaches, when it really could fly if the time needed to be made up for any reason. One BUT set also did duty on the Harrow–Belmont branch, and on other similar lightly-loaded branch lines. They suffered from many of the operating problems of the other DMU bogie vehicles as well as poor ride qualities, and problems in working track circuits.

For some six years there were no more ventures in the two axle passenger car stock, but in 1958 a further 22 were produced by five different manufacturers, for use on branch lines of which it was said that they could not be run economically with current types of diesel trains.

The first of these railbuses to be delivered was built by Associated Commercial Cars Limited (once called Auto-Carriers) better known as AC Cars of Thames Ditton, a maker of sports cars, one of which had won the Monte Carlo Rally in 1926, and the first firm to produce an aluminium engine block. Its railbus was fitted with an AEC 150hp diesel engine driving through the standard transmission system, and providing 46 seats in a weight of 11 tons. It was tested on the Western Region in February 1958, allocated the number W79979 and was promptly transferred to the Scottish Region, where it was re-numbered with the SC prefix. The other four cars in the batch were delayed owing to a fire in the works, but later went into service on the Western Region and, based at Swindon, worked the Kemble to Cirencester and Tetbury branches until April 1964. After that they worked from Bodmin and Yeovil until January 1967, when they too went to Scotland. After a year there they were withdrawn, when all railbus operation ceased on 27 January 1968, outlived by the last months of steam locomotive operation.

Of the five AC Railbuses, three remain in existence W79976 is at Bleadon & Uphill in the care of the West Somerset Museum. W79978 is now earning its keep on the Kent & East Sussex Railway, having been for 13 years on the North Yorkshire Moors Railway. SC79979 is staying in Scotland in the care of the Strathspey Railway, having at one time lost all its working parts. It owed its salvation to the fact that its resting place at Craigentinny was needed for the new HST Depot, from where it was sold as scrap.

The second batch of railbuses to be delivered to BR comprised five built by Waggon and Mäschinenbau of Donauworth. They were fitted with Buessing 150hp engines, running at 1900rpm driving through a ZF 6-speed electro-magnetic gearbox. Later, three of these, starting with E79963 had type A220X AEC engines installed. These vehicles weighed 15 tons and seated 56 passengers. They were based on Cambridge for work in the Fenland areas and were withdrawn in 1964 after their operational branches had been closed by the Beeching cuts. Two went to the North Norfolk Railway (E79960 and E79963) while two more went to the Keighley & Worth Valley Railway. M79964 had been for a time with the LM Region on the Miller's Dale branch, and E79962 went direct from Cambridge. The fifth car (M79961) which had also joined the LM Region, was scrapped at Rotherham in 1968.

Park Royal Vehicles supplied five cars in July 1958, which had AEC 150hp engines and standard transmission. They weighed 15 tons and provided 50 seats. Starting life on the LM Region they all went to Scotland in 1960, where they saw duty around

BUT 4-wheel railcar set; the original unit built in 1952 was delivered in grey livery but all the cars in the three sets were painted in BR green as seen here

Wickham 4-wheel railbus, No SC79965, supplied to the Scottish Region of British Railways. (*D. Wickham & Co Ltd*)

Track recording coach built by D. Wickham & Co. (*D. Wickham & Co*)

Diagrams showing the measuring equipment on the Wickham track recording car.

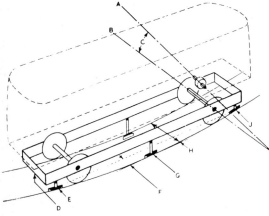

FIG. 1 (LEFT).—DIAGRAM SHOWING THE MEASUREMENTS OF CURVATURE

A, gyro spin axis (horizontal datum)
B, axle
C, cant
D, probe-carrying frame
E, sensing shoe
F, versine measurement of curvature
G, sensing shoe
H, gauge
J, sensing shoe

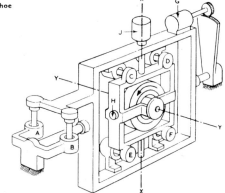

FIG. 3 (ABOVE).—HORIZONTAL GYROSCOPIC DATUM FOR CANT MEASUREMENT

A, B, torque motors to keep spin axis, Y-Y, across the vehicle
C, D, torque motors compensate for centrifugal force on offset weight, H
E, F, torque motors correct for earth's rotation effect in plane of cant measurement
G, pick-off for angle between floor and spin axis Y-Y (angle between floor and axle added electrically)
H, offset weight which precesses gyro until axis, X-X, is vertical
J, A. C. pick-off operates torque motors (A, B)

FIG 2 (BELOW).—SUCCESSIVE POSITIONS OF SENSING SHOE IN NEGOTIATING CROSSING

A, sensing shoe approaching gap at crossing. Guide shoe has entered flangeway between opposite running rail and check rail
B, guide shoe in contact with check rail prevents sensing shoe taking wrong route at gap
C, sensing shoe has picked up again on running rail before guide shoe leaves check rail
D, tie bar contains compression member for negotiation of single-bladed catch points

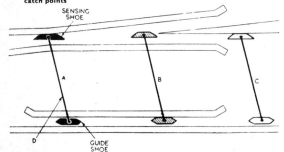

SENSING SHOE

GUIDE SHOE

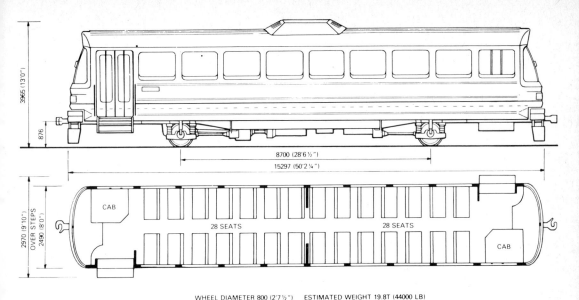

8700 (28'6½")
15297 (50'2¼")
3965 (13'0")
876
2970 (9'10")
OVER STEPS
2490 (8'0")

CAB

28 SEATS

28 SEATS

CAB

WHEEL DIAMETER 800 (2'7½")   ESTIMATED WEIGHT 19.8T (44000 LB)

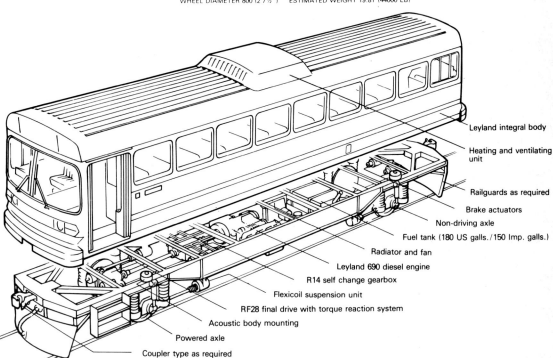

Leyland integral body
Heating and ventilating unit
Railguards as required
Brake actuators
Non-driving axle
Fuel tank (180 US galls./150 Imp. galls.)
Radiator and fan
Leyland 690 diesel engine
R14 self change gearbox
Flexicoil suspension unit
RF28 final drive with torque reaction system
Acoustic body mounting
Powered axle
Coupler type as required

Layout of Wickham-built LEV R3. (*D. Wickham & Co Ltd*)

Arrochar, Ayr and Alloa, and were withdrawn in 1968. The body from SC79971 was later seen at Millerhill.

The five supplied by D. Wickham & Company of Ware were the lightest at 11.2 tons, and seated 44 passengers. These were equipped with Meadows 105hp engine type 6HDT500, running at 1,800rpm, driving through a Freeborn–Wickham disc-and-ring coupling to a self-changing 4-speed Wilson type R11E gearbox.

These vehicles incorporated the Wickham tubular system of body construction with a separate tubular underframe on which the body was flexibly mounted. The axle boxes were not in horn guides, but controlled by a radius arm with semi-elliptic springs and Woodhead-Monroe hydraulic shock-absorbers. The doors were air-operated from the driver's cab, or by local control. The last of the cars (SC79969) was equipped with pneumatic suspension by André and Westinghouse in the form of air bags in place of the springs used in the other four cars, Nos SC79965–8. The pressure in these air springs varied according to the load between 44lb/sq in 74lb/sq in with a surge

Wickham-built LEV model R3, based on the Leyland National bus body, seen here on the Boston & Maine Railroad, USA. (*D. Wickham & Co Ltd*)

tank for damping purposes. The five were allocated to the Scottish Region in 1958, but the one with the air springs was withdrawn in 1963 as a result of a mishap; two more were laid-up in 1964 and disposed of with the others in 1968.

The last of the 22 were a couple built by Bristol Commercial Vehicles, a subsidiary of the Bristol Aero Engine Company, with bodywork by Eastern Coach Works and fitted with a Gardner 6HLW engine giving

R3 type railbus, as built by British Rail Engineering Ltd (BREL) and used on the Western Region before going to Northern Ireland. (*British Rail*)

112hp at 1,700rpm, probably the best engine of the lot. These cars weighed 13.5 tons and seating 56 passengers. They spent their 10-year life in Scotland, being withdrawn and scrapped in 1968.

A final similar product of that era was one by D. Wickham for track recording duty, No DB999507. Since an adequate axle load was desirable for this duty the frame was of standard fabricated construction with buffers and drawgear. There was also a lattice-girder frame for carrying the probes for gauge and curvature measurements, supported at the axle boxes. Cant was also measured by the use of a gyroscope mounted above the free axle. The recording equipment was made by Elliott Brothers Limited, which also designed the vehicle layout. This car was heavier than the buses at

Prototype Class 140 railbus unit. (*British Rail*)

24 tons, and since the maximum speed was only 55mph the Meadows engine was derated to 97hp. This vehicle was withdrawn in 1970.

The New Railbus Concept

After a gap of nearly six years from the general railbus demise, a decision was taken in 1974 to investigate a 2-axle vehicle based on the work undertaken at Derby in connection with high-speed freight vehicle suspension and ride. This was further investigated by Leyland Vehicles in 1976 and a design undertaken in 1977.

The vehicle was based on a body designed by Leyland to be resiliently-mounted on a chassis fitted with flexicoil suspension on two axles spaced 7.35m apart. This was built and carried out trials under tow in 1978 at up to 95mph (150kph). Power equipment then was installed, consisting of a Leyland 200hp (150kW) engine with a 4-speed gearbox. In 1979 this vehicle, designated R1 or Leyland Experimental Vehicle (LEV), carried out trials on the the Old Dalby test track at up to 80mph.

Later that year, through the offices of Transmark Ltd., LEV was tested out in the USA on the Boston & Maine Railroad between Boston (North) and Concord, where on Class 3 track with staggered rail joints it was run successfully at up to 56mph. It also ran on the North East Corridor line between Boston (South) and Attleborough on Class 6 welded track at up to 72mph. As a result of this venture an order was received for a larger version of LEV and this model, designated R3, was assembled by D. Wickham & Company and delivered to the USA in October 1980.

The R3 had a 56-seat steel body with an aluminium alloy roof, insulated and lined with plastic laminate sheets, and it was mounted on four resilient pads. There is a driver's cab at each end and the air-operated double leaf doors are at the body ends at opposite corners.

At that time the LEV was tried out in the Eastern Region between Ipswich and Lowestoft for a period of two months, following which a second R3 was built by BREL in conjunction with Leyland Vehicles. That car ran on the Western Region between Bristol and Severn Beach for eight months from October 1981 and was then converted to 1.6m (5ft 3in) gauge and sold to Northern Ireland.

That R3 is 15.3m long and has a chassis capable of taking end loads of 100 tonnes. The engine, a Leyland

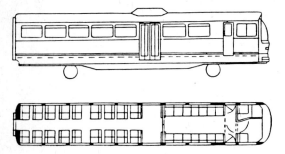

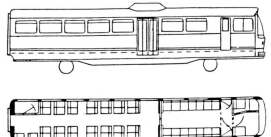

Diagram of the Class 141 2-car railbus set

690 diesel, drives through an R14 self-change gearbox to an RF28 final drive on an axle with 800mm diameter wheels. The brakes are of the wheel tread type with two composition blocks per wheel, pneumatically controlled from a commercial vehicle type actuator incorporating a spring-loaded emergency system.

The coach heating is primarily from the engine cooling water with a separate oil-fired heater as a backup. The heating and ventilating unit is roof-mounted with washable polyurethane foam air filters, and having a fresh air ratio controllable between 80 and 100 percent. The seating capacity of 56 is provided by standard Leyland National bus seats, and entry is through the standard National double jack-knife type F door, weighing 72kg. The driver's cabs at each end are securely partitioned-off for safety, and have the railway type of hand controls; there are standard bus windscreen wipers and washers. The designed maximum speed is 75mph, and the tare weight is 19.8 tonnes

Proposed design for Metro-Cammell Class 142 railbus. (*Metro Cammell*)

While the development of the R3 type railbus was proceeding primarily with a view to export potential, it was appreciated that some services in the UK would need more capacity than could be provided in a single vehicle that could not be worked in multiple. It was also considered that a 2-axle car that could be built more on the UK railway pattern and worked in multiples of up to eight cars could replace many of the older DMUs on branch lines.

Accordingly in 1981 BREL produced a twin railbus, Class 140, which employed many of the components used in the R3 model. These vehicles had the traditional level floor throughout, suitable to the UK platform height, with sliding doors of the swing-plug type. A steel plate under the body floor was provided as a fire barrier and to reduce engine noise. A new reversing gearbox, type RRE 5, was introduced in order to eliminate manual gear-changing and the final-drive dog clutch, both of which caused trouble in the former DMU fleet.

This pair of Class 140 railbuses was designed with corridor connections at both ends of each car and with the standard BR high-backed seat considered more suitable for long journeys. This has not proved so acceptable to the public and will not be used in the next design of railbus, Class 141. The Class 140 vehicles

Wickham built LEV Model R3, as supplied to the Boston & Maine RR

were given an extensive tour of BR in 1981 and in June were tried out in the Bradford area, since investigations in 1979 had shown that 80 out of 96 local peak period trains were either 2- or 3-car sets, and the Class 140 was considered suitable for this type of duty.

Each car was fitted with a Leyland turbocharged diesel engine type TL80 giving 218hp (163kW) at 2,100rpm and driving through a 19in fluid flywheel to a RRE5 MkIII reversing gearbox having four speeds with ratios of 4.25/1, 2.41/1, 1.59/1 and 1/1. The final drive, type RF42 had a ratio of 2.33/1. Gearbox and final drive were built by Self-Changing Gear Co.

Resulting from the trials of the LEV, the R3, and the Class 140 vehicles, and taking into account passenger reaction a batch of twenty 2-car units (Class 141) is under construction at the time this book closed for press embracing the best of the features so far tried.

Passenger reaction and measurements showed the

R3 as having the lowest noise level (72dB at 60mph) compared with 82 for Class 140 and 78 for a DMU, both at 75mph. The adverse comment for the R3 was due to the platform gap for the steps that had to be provided for access from lower levels, otherwise both the R3 and Class 140 were preferred to the ageing DMU stock.

In arriving at the final design, this had to include the ability to work on both main and rural lines with journeys of up to 100 miles and to be able to operate for two weeks away from its own depot. It had to be cheap initially and low on fuel and maintenance costs, reliable and pleasing in ride and appearance. Initially it is not intended to multiple with existing DMUs because they had vacuum brakes which will not be used on the Class 141 stock.

The Class 141s are built in 2-car units with a driving cab at each end, but without corridors past the driver. In 2-car units with a corridor between the two cars provision can be made for toilets, luggage, perambulators and bicycles in one of the cars. The body will be on four resilient mountings and the seats will be the low bus type which seem the more popular. Doors will be an improved pattern of the bus folding type and the heater unit will be roof-mounted as on the R3 vehicles. The full width windscreen is to be of high-impact laminate glass to protect the driver from missiles. As on the Southern DEMUs two batteries will be provided, one for engine starting only; it is interesting that the Leyland body width is 8ft 2½in.

On the Class 140 unit wheelspin proved a problem since the driver could not know if it was occurring on the other car, and on the Class 141 cars speed probes will be provided on each axle; wheelslip detection will automatically cause a change to a higher gear.

The first pair of Class 141 railbus units, 141.001, consisting of DMS vehicles No 55502 and 55522 were handed over by BREL to BR on 22 September 1983 at Litchurch Lane, Derby. These units are believed to be heavier than originally designed because of changes in the chassis design to allow for the power unit to be removed horizontally by fork lift trucks in maintenance depots. The first set was put on exhibition at Leeds on 28 September and entered service in the area of the West Yorkshire Passenger Transport Authority where it was due to be joined by the further nineteen pairs of 2-car Class 141 units as they come off the production line.

If the design proves popular and effective it could provide a basis for further DMU replacements, but early in 1984 BR was authorised to order seventy-five 2-car units designated Class 142 and called for tenders from five manufacturers. Clearly the 141 design as such might not be repeated and the way seemed open for other ideas to be added to the experience gained from LEV, Class 140 and Class 141 railbuses.

The railbus obviously has a future and alongside the more conventional bogie units and Inter-City 125 HSTs means that the railcar train from its early beginnings 80 years ago as a cheap substitute for a conventional steam train will in future provide in its various forms by far the greatest percentage of passenger services on non-electrified lines in Britain well into the next century.

Index